Unix for Oracle DBAs
Pocket Reference

Unix for Oracle DBAs
Pocket Reference

Donald K. Burleson

O'REILLY®

Beijing • Cambridge • Farnham • Köln • Paris • Sebastopol • Taipei • Tokyo

Unix for Oracle DBAs Pocket Reference

by Donald K. Burleson

Copyright © 2001 O'Reilly & Associates, Inc. All rights reserved.
Printed in the United States of America.

Published by O'Reilly & Associates, Inc., 101 Morris Street,
Sebastopol, CA 95472.

Editor: Jonathan Gennick

Production Editor: Emily Quill

Cover Designer: Ellie Volckhausen

Printing History:

        January 2001:   First Edition.

0-596-00066-9   [5/01]
[C]

Table of Contents

Unix for Oracle DBAs
Pocket Reference

Introduction

The *Unix for Oracle DBAs Pocket Reference* is a quick reference describing the Unix commands most often used by Oracle database administrators. It's the result of my 20 years of accumulating Unix tips and techniques. For each of the commands included in this book, I've provided the basic syntax and a short, illustrative example. This guide also contains many short Unix scripts that should save you dozens of hours of manual effort.

I've organized the commands and examples in this book into the following major topic areas:

Understanding Unix
Gives you a little bit of the history of Unix and tells you some things that you need to know regarding case sensitivity, safety, and shells.

Building Unix Commands
Describes the process of creating complex Unix commands for Oracle.

Unix Server Environment
Describes the commands that make Unix easier for DBAs.

Process Management
Describes the basic Unix commands you use to display and manage server processes.

Server Values

Shows you how to display relevant server values in Unix.

Memory and CPU Management

Shows the main commands used to display information about memory segments, swap space, and semaphores used by an Oracle database. Also covers commands used to monitor CPU utilization.

Semaphore Management

Shows you how to monitor semaphore usage by your Oracle server and how to remove semaphore sets for an instance that has crashed.

System Log Messages

Shows you how to view operating-system log files.

Server Monitoring

Describes the details of using the server utilities *vmstat*, *sar*, and *glance*.

File Management

Describes commands that assist in file management tasks.

Disk Management

Shows you how to get information about the disks on your system. This section includes commands to list physical volumes, logical volumes, and mount points.

Miscellaneous Shell Scripts

Presents a number of shell scripts that I've found to be useful over the years, but that don't fit into any of the other sections.

Writing this pocket reference was especially challenging because of the dialect differences between the major implementations of Unix. For example, commands in HP-UX are often different from those in Sun Solaris. I've emphasized commands that are common to all Unix dialects. Where differences occur, I've attempted to cover the following

---

platforms: HP-UX, IBM AIX, and Sun Solaris. You'll also find some specific dialect commands for IRIX and DEC Unix.

In addition to experimenting with the commands shown in this book, I encourage you to read more about them in books such as *Unix in a Nutshell* by Arnold Robbins (O'Reilly). Also, remember that the online Unix manpages are a great source of information about Unix commands. For example, to learn about the *cat* command, enter *man cat* at the command prompt.

Acknowledgments

This type of book requires the dedicated efforts of many people, and I have worked closely as a team with many others who have supported this effort. Foremost, I need to acknowledge the efforts of my wife, Janet Burleson, whose impatience with Unix syntax led to the development of this book.

This book certainly would not have been possible without a tremendous amount of hard work and support from the staff of O'Reilly & Associates. In particular, I would like to express my thanks to Jonathan Gennick, one of the Oracle Series editors, whose dedication to quality added a great deal of value to this text. Jonathan provided countless hours of work editing and improving each section in this book.

Three technical reviewers also contributed generously of their time and efforts in order to make this a better book. My thanks to Dan Hardin, John-Paul Navarro, and Joseph Testa for their many comments and suggestions.

Ellie Volckhausen designed the cover, and I want to thank her (I think) for giving me the fly book. It's certainly a memorable distinction. Flies are annoying, as is Unix at times. It's my sincere hope that after reading this book you will find Unix to be much less annoying than any pesky fly.

Conventions Used in This Book

It is important to remember that all Unix commands are case-sensitive and should be entered exactly as displayed in this text.

The following conventions are used in this book:

Italics
> Used for script, file, and directory names, variables, utilities, commands in text, and new terms where defined.

`Constant Width`
> Used for code examples.

`Constant Width Italics`
> In some code examples, indicates an element (e.g., a filename) that you supply.

`Constant Width Bold`
> Used to indicate user input in code examples.

[] In syntax examples, square brackets enclose optional items.

TIP

Indicates a tip, suggestion, or general note. For example, I'll tell you if you need to use a particular Unix version, or if an operation requires certain privileges.

WARNING

Indicates a warning or caution. For example, I'll tell you if Unix does not behave as you'd expect, or if a particular operation has a negative impact on performance.

Long Code Lines

One aspect of Unix that caused my editor and me much consternation as we worked on this book was the problem

---

of dealing with long Unix code lines in a narrow book format. When you start combining several Unix commands together as one large compound command, you quickly exceed the 50 characters or so that fit on one printed line in this book. Tabular output from the various monitoring utilities also typically exceeds 50 characters in width. After much discussion and debate, we came up with some solutions. Our approach to handling long code lines recognizes the following four categories:

- Long commands introduced by preceding text
- Long commands in input/output examples
- Wide columnar output
- Unix script examples

Long commands that appear by themselves, and that are introduced by preceding text, are simply allowed to wrap to the width of the printed line. For example:

```
ps -ef|grep "ora_"|grep -v grep|grep
$ORACLE_SID|awk '{print $2}'|xargs kill -9
```

In these cases, it's usually obvious from the context that the multiple printed lines really represent one long Unix command.

Similarly, I allow commands to wrap in input/output examples, as shown here:

```
>ps -ef|grep "ora_"|grep -v grep|grep
$ORACLE_SID|awk '{ print $2 }'

17748
18134
```

In these input/output examples, user input is shown in bold, and the prompt appears non-bold at the front of each input line. These visual cues make it reasonably obvious when a line has wrapped because of page width limitations.

Wide, columnar output presented the greatest challenge. An 80-column report simply looks ugly if each line is allowed to wrap separately. I take one of two approaches to columnar output, depending on whether I need to keep all or only some of the columns. When it's not important for you to see every column of output, I snip a few columns out of the middle in order to make things fit. Notice the horizontal ellipses in the following example, which mark the location of one or more missing columns:

```
-rwxr-xr-x   1 oracle   dba ...   09:11 a.ksh*
-rwxr-xr-x   1 oracle   dba ...   09:11 lert.ksh*
```

Where it's important that you see all of the columns, I split the output into two blocks, and I stack those blocks on top of each other. For example:

```
Filesystem   1024-blks     Free   %Used...
/dev/hd4        32768     11636     65%...
/dev/hd2       802816     15920     99%...

...      Iu    %Iu   Mounted on
...    2017    13%   /
...   26308    14%   /usr
```

Here, the trailing ellipses at the end of the first three lines indicate where you would normally see more columns. Those columns are then shown separately, with leading ellipses to indicate the continuation.

Using these two methods, I hope I've made the columnar output as readable as possible given the small size of this book.

Scripts represent the last area of concern. I've included many small scripts in this book, and some of the commands in those scripts are quite long. Fortunately, I have some control of line width and format when writing a script. To provide reliable visual cues of when a long line wraps, I've chosen to make use of the Unix continuation character, which is a backslash (\). When you see it at the end of a long line, you know that the subsequent line is a continuation of the first. Here's an example:

```
if [ -z "$2" ]
then
    echo "Usage: mon_purge.ksh <ORACLE_SID>\
  <#_days> (where value is > 100)"
    exit 99
fi
```

In this *if* statement, the *echo* command is one long command. When you type in scripts from this book, you can enter them exactly as shown, including the backslash characters. Unix will recognize the backslashes and reassemble the continued commands before executing them. The following two commands, for example, are identical as far as Unix is concerned:

```
echo "Hello world"
echo "Hello\
  world"
```

When I continue commands, any leading spaces you see in a continuation line are significant. In this example, there is one space between the words "Hello" and "world".

Understanding Unix

Unix is an operating system. It's been developed over the past 30 years by several different vendors. This book can't hope to be a tutorial on the use of Unix. I assume that you know enough to log into your Unix system, get a command prompt, and issue commands. Even so, there are some important things to review before you get started with this book.

History

The history of Unix goes back to 1969, when the first versions of Unix were developed by AT&T's Bell Labs. The operating system had a certain elegance, was freely available, and quickly caught on with vendors of minicomputer systems who needed an operating system for the hardware that they were selling.

As different vendors adopted Unix, they each began to create their own, slightly unique versions of the operating system. Today, you have HP-UX, Sun Solaris, IBM AIX, and a number of other variants to deal with.

Linux is a Unix-like operating system first put together by Linus Torvalds in 1991 because he needed an operating system for his PC and could not afford any of the commercial Unix variants of that day. Linux has gone on to achieve phenomenal growth and is widely used today as a server operating system on x86 machines. Linux is also available for the PowerPC, Sparc, IBM S/390, and Amiga.

Most commonly used Unix commands work more or less identically on all Unix and Linux platforms. The *ls* command, which lists files in a directory, is an example of such a command. I've never seen a Unix or Linux version that did not support *ls*. There are a number of command options available with *ls*, however, and not all options are available on all platforms.

System management commands probably represent the area where you will run into the greatest number of differences between the Unix variants on the market. These are the commands used to display information about disks, memory, and performance. Most Unix users are not bothered by this problem, but unfortunately, these commands are the ones that you as the database administrator (DBA) will most likely need to use.

Unless specified otherwise, I've used only commonly available commands and options in this book. Where platform differences exist, I've attempted to cover all the platforms listed in the introduction. Sometimes a command available on one platform does not have an analog on another. I've noted this in the text where appropriate.

Case Sensitivity

Unix commands often consist of cryptic abbreviations and acronyms, and they are always case-sensitive. Command options are case-sensitive as well. People who have "grown up" using Unix simply accept this as the way things are, but it can be a major stumbling block for people making the transition to Unix from other operating systems.

The vast majority of Unix commands are lowercase. The command to list files, for example, is *ls*. As you can see, you can enter *ls* in lowercase and get results, but if you try using uppercase, you'll get an error:

```
>ls
listener.ora  sqlnet.log        tnsnames.ora

>LS
bash: LS: command not found
```

Unix commands support a wide variety of command options that allow you to fine-tune their behavior. Command options are introduced by a hyphen following the command, and they usually consist of one letter. Like commands, options are case-sensitive. For example, use *ls −c*, and you'll get a list of files in your current directory that is sorted by creation date. Use *ls −C*, and you'll get a columnar listing of files.

Safety

Some operating systems attempt to protect you from making a serious mistake. Often this protection takes the form of an "are you sure?" prompt. Unix does no such thing. A key design philosophy behind Unix is to assume that you, the user, know exactly what you are doing at all times. Thus, if you log in as the root user, Unix will allow you to use a simple command such as *rm −rf* * to wipe out all files on every disk and filesystem connected to your server. You won't be prompted for confirmation. Unix will simply delete everything.

Usually, you are protected from such disastrous consequences as deleting your entire disk by Unix privileges and file protections. No sane Unix administrator logs in as root unless root privileges are specifically required. This is the reason that all Oracle installs are done as the Unix Oracle user. Most users have access to only their own files. Still, when working in Unix, it pays to be careful. Be certain that you understand what a command is going to do *before* you issue it. When first using a new and potentially dangerous command, consider trying it out on a test system before you try it on your production servers.

Linkability

Another guiding design philosophy of Unix is that commands should be simple, should do one thing well, and should be capable of linking with other commands. Because of this design, commands are frequently not issued by themselves, but rather in conjunction with one or more others. Each command performs one task, and then feeds its output to the next command. The following example shows *cat* and *grep* being used to extract information about the Oracle SID named *prod* from the */etc/oratab* file:

```
>cat /etc/oratab | grep prod
prod:/s01/app/oracle/product/8.1.6:Y
```

TIP

There are many examples in this book that reference the *oratab* file. In AIX and HP-UX, *oratab* is located in the */etc* directory. In Solaris, the *oratab* file is located in the */var/opt/oracle* directory.

In this instance, *cat* types out the entire file. That output feeds into the *grep* command, which filters out everything but the line containing the word "prod". Commands such as this that are linked together can sometimes be quite long and intimidating. You'll learn more in the section titled "Building Unix Commands."

Shells

You'll often hear the term "shell" in connection with Unix. A Unix *shell* is a program that allows you to enter commands and see results. The bash shell is one of the most commonly used Unix shells. Other shells include csh and Korn. For consistency, all of the shell scripts are written for the Korn shell, one of the most popular Unix shells.

Unix commands function identically under different shells, but shells also sometimes have commands of their own. All the commands in this book should work regardless of which shell you are using. The one area where you may be affected is described in the later section "Unix Server Environment," where I talk about placing commands in a startup script that is executed when you first log on to your server. Not all shells use the same filename for the startup script.

Building Unix Commands

One of the most confounding things for the Unix neophyte is being confronted with a complex Unix command. The cryptic nature of Unix is such that even the most seasoned Unix professional may have trouble deciphering such a command. Hidden in that complexity, however, is a great deal of power. In order to leverage that power for your day-to-day work, it's essential for you to learn how to deal with complex commands.

In this section, we will begin by examining a cryptic Unix command in order to see how it is really composed of many simpler commands. We'll then walk through the process of creating such a command in order to perform a specific task.

Regarding the terms *commands* and *scripts*, you should note that any command may become a script if it is encapsulated into a file for execution. Hence, *find . –print* can be a command if executed from the prompt, or a script if placed into a file.

Decompose a Complex Unix Command

This section shows how a Unix programmer can string commands together into a powerful one-line command. The following one-line Unix script performs an important Oracle function—it kills all Oracle background processes when the database cannot be shut down normally:

```
ps -ef|grep "ora_"|grep -v grep|awk '{ print $2
}'|xargs kill -9
```

At first glance, this Unix command appears to be a conglomeration of cryptic letters. However, this is actually a series of commands that are joined together using the pipe operator (|). Here's a view of the command that's a bit easier to follow:

```
ps -ef
|
grep "ora_"
|
grep -v grep
|
awk '{ print $2 }'
|
xargs kill -9
```

The pipe symbol tells Unix to use the output from one command as input to the next command. For example, you can pipe the output from *ps –ef* as input to *grep "ora_"*. The output from *ps –ef* is a list of all processes on the server; this is passed to *grep "ora_"* to filter out only the Oracle processes running on the server. With that in mind, you can examine the commands one at a time and see how each successive command refines the output from the previous one.

Build a Complex Unix Command from Scratch

Now that you've seen how a complex, one-line script is really composed of several simpler commands connected by the pipe operator (|), it's time to take a look at this from the opposite standpoint. I'll walk you through a couple of case studies showing how to start with a goal in mind, and build up a one-line script to accomplish that goal. I'll start by showing you how to build a one-line script to kill all the Oracle processes on your server. Then I'll show you how to build a one-line script to find files that contain a specific text string.

WARNING

Be sure to read the earlier section titled "Long Code Lines." That explains how I've chosen to represent code lines in this book when they are too long to fit on one printed line.

A script to kill all Oracle processes

In this example, you will see how to write a one-line Unix script to kill all Oracle background processes for a database. This is a common Unix script used by Oracle DBAs when a database is locked up, and Server Manager cannot be used to stop the database in a more "gentle" fashion.

To begin, the Unix *kill* command is used to kill a process. The basic format of the *kill* command is as follows:

```
kill -9 PID1 PID2 PID3...PIDn
```

PID1 through *PIDn* represent the list of process IDs for the processes that you want to kill. The −9 option directs Unix to kill the processes immediately. The trick is to be able to identify and kill only the Oracle processes. That's done by stringing several commands together. The resulting one-line script looks like this:

```
ps -ef|grep "ora_"|grep -v grep|grep
$ORACLE_SID|awk '{print $2}'|xargs kill -9
```

Don't spend too much time up front trying to figure out just how this command works. I'll walk you through the process of building it. To begin, you want to get a list of active processes on the server. You can do that using the following command:

```
ps -ef
```

If you execute *ps –ef* on your server, you'll see a long list of processes—both for Oracle and for many other things. However, you want to limit your output to only those processes that are related to the Oracle database. The *grep* command can be used to do this. Oracle background process names always begin with "ora_", so piping the output of *ps –ef* through *grep "ora_"* will remove all but the Oracle background processes. For example:

```
>ps -ef|grep "ora_"

    oracle 13022     1   0   May 07 ...   ora_db02_vald
    oracle 14796 42726   0 09:00:46  0:00 grep ora_
    oracle 17778     1   0   May 07 ...   ora_smon_devp
    oracle 18134     1   0   May 07 ...   ora_snp1_vald
    oracle 19516     1   0   May 07 ...   ora_db04_prod
    oracle 21114     1   0   May 07 ...   ora_snp0_devp
    oracle 28436     1   0   May 07 ...   ora_arch_prod
    oracle 17748     1   0   May 07 ...   ora_smon_prod
    oracle 18134     1   0   May 07 ...   ora_snp1_prod
    oracle 12516     1   0   May 07 ...   ora_pmon_prod
    oracle 21714     1   0   May 07 ...   ora_reco_prod
    oracle 21814     1   0   May 07 ...   ora_dbwr_prod
```

One thing you'll notice about this output is that it includes the process that's running the *grep* command. Pipe this output through *grep –v grep* to remove the *grep* command, so you don't kill your own process. The *–v* option makes *grep* work in a way that's opposite its usual manner. Whereas *grep* finds and includes strings, *grep –v* excludes strings. In this next example, you'll see that the *grep* line is now missing from the output:

```
>ps -ef|grep "ora_"|grep -v grep
```

```
oracle 13022    1    0    May 07 ...    ora_db02_vald
oracle 17778    1    0    May 07 ...    ora_smon_devp
oracle 18134    1    0    May 07 ...    ora_snp1_vald
oracle 19516    1    0    May 07 ...    ora_db04_prod
oracle 21114    1    0    May 07 ...    ora_snp0_devp
oracle 28436    1    0    May 07 ...    ora_arch_prod
oracle 17748    1    0    May 07 ...    ora_smon_prod
oracle 18134    1    0    May 07 ...    ora_snp1_prod
oracle 12516    1    0    May 07 ...    ora_pmon_prod
oracle 21714    1    0    May 07 ...    ora_reco_prod
oracle 21814    1    0    May 07 ...    ora_dbwr_prod
```

Next, you should filter out all processes except those for the current *ORACLE_SID*. That way you delete the background processes only for that one instance instead of for all instances. Do that by grepping for the *SID* name:

```
>ps -ef|grep "ora"|grep -v grep|grep
$ORACLE_SID

oracle 17748    1    0    May 07 ...    ora_smon_prod
oracle 18134    1    0    May 07 ...    ora_snp1_prod
oracle 12516    1    0    May 07 ...    ora_pmon_prod
oracle 21714    1    0    May 07 ...    ora_reco_prod
oracle 21814    1    0    May 07 ...    ora_dbwr_prod
```

Now that you have an accurate list of processes that you want to kill, you can use the *awk* command to get the process ID (PID) for each of these processes. The PID is in the second column, so use the *awk '{print $2}'* command to display only that column:

```
>ps -ef|grep "ora_"|grep -v grep|grep
$ORACLE_SID|awk '{ print $2 }'

17748
18134
12516
21714
21814
```

Now you have a list of process ID numbers for the Oracle background processes. For the last step, you use the *xargs* command to pipe this list of PIDs to the *kill* command. For example:

```
ps -ef|grep "ora_"|grep -v grep|grep
$ORACLE_SID|awk '{ print $2 }'|xargs kill -9
```

Now that you've created this compound command, you can assign it to a Unix alias so that you can execute it with a single, short command.

TIP

Not all shells support aliases. For example, if you are using the Bourne shell, you will not be able to use aliases.

The following command assigns the new compound command to an alias named *nuke_oracle*:

```
alias nuke_oracle="ps -ef|grep 'ora_'|grep -v grep|grep
$ORACLE_SID|awk '{ print $2 }'|xargs kill -9"
```

By placing the command to create the alias in your *.profile* file, you'll have it available every time you sign on to Unix. By using an alias, you encapsulate the command without the burden of placing the command into a script file. Now, entering the alias *nuke_oracle* at the command prompt will cause your command to run, which will kill all Oracle background processes for the instance to which *$ORACLE_SID* points.

A script to find all files containing a specific string

In Unix, it is not easy to find files that contain specific strings. This section explores a way to quickly build a command that will allow you to find a file that contains a particular character string.

Using commands such as *xargs*, you can quickly generate Unix scripts to perform many useful tasks. Suppose that in the past you have written an SQL script that queries the DBA_2PC_PENDING view. Unfortunately, you have completely forgotten the name and location of the script file, and you need a Unix command to locate it. The example in this section demonstrates how you can leverage the *xargs* command to quickly create a complex command that searches for your lost file.

Begin by writing a command that will display all filenames on the server. This syntax is quite simple in Unix, as the *find* command can be used to return a list of every file on the server starting from your current directory:

```
>find . -print

/home/oracle/sqlnet.log
/home/oracle/export.sh
/home/oracle/mon
/home/oracle/mon/a.ksh
/home/oracle/mon/alert.ksh
/home/oracle/mon/count.ksh
/home/oracle/mon/create_mon1_tables.ksh
/home/oracle/mon/fix_db.ksh
/home/oracle/mon/get_vmstat.ksh
/home/oracle/mon/oracheck.lst
/home/oracle/mon/alerts_PROD.lst
/home/oracle/mon/mail_reports.ksh
```

TIP

The dot in the *find* . command tells the system to start at the current directory (dot) and work its way down the file hierarchy from this directory. If you want to see all of the files on your server, issue *cd /* to switch to the root directory prior to running the *find* command.

You now have a complete list of all the Unix files under your current directory. The next step is to pipe this list of filenames to the *grep* command to search for files containing the string DBA_2PC_PENDING. Because the *grep* command accepts a filename as an argument, you can use *xargs* to execute a *grep* command to search each file for the string you need:

```
find . -print|xargs grep -i dba_2pc_pending
```

The *-i* option tells *grep* to ignore case. You can execute this new command at the Unix prompt, and you'll see that it quickly finds the file you are seeking:

```
>find . -print|xargs grep -i dba_2pc_pending
```

```
home/oracle/sql/pending.sql:   dba_2pc_pending
```

This ability to take a basic Unix command and pipe the output into another command is a fundamental principle of Unix shell programming for Oracle.

Unix Server Environment

This section presents handy Unix commands that will make it easier for you to navigate in your Unix environment. The first part of this section looks at commands that can be automatically executed when you sign on to Unix as the Oracle user. There is a special file in your home directory in which you can place Unix commands that you want automatically executed when you sign on to the system. If you use the Korn shell, this file is named *.profile*. If you use the C shell, it will be called *.cshrc*. If there's any doubt, your Unix system administrator will be able to tell you the name of the file in your particular environment.

Also in this section, you will see how to create a standard Unix prompt, wrap SQL in a Unix script, and write a utility to quickly change all files in a directory. In addition, you will explore submitting background jobs and sending mail from Unix, and you'll use the powerful *rsh* command to make a script that visits multiple databases on multiple servers.

Set a Standard Unix Prompt

Placing the following code snippet in your *.profile* file will give you a Unix prompt that identifies your current server name, database name, and working directory. Knowing this information can help prevent you from accidentally running a command against the wrong database. Note that I have my prompt go to a new line after displaying the information, so that I have a full 79 characters in which to type my Unix commands.

```
#************************************************
# Standard Unix Prompt
#************************************************
PS1="
`hostname`*\${ORACLE_SID}-\${PWD}
>"
```

Here is what the prompt looks like after you have executed the *PS1* command shown in the previous example. Note how the prompt changes when you change directories.

```
corphp*PROD-/home/oracle
>pwd

/home/oracle

corphp*PROD-/home/oracle
>cd /u01/oradata/PROD

corphp*PROD-/u01/oradata/PROD
>
```

Create Useful Unix Aliases for Oracle

This section shows you how you can place a list of helpful Unix aliases in the *.profile* file of a Unix Oracle user.

An alias is a Unix shortcut whereby you can define a short name to use in place of a long Unix command. For example, you could create a shortcut called "log" that would execute the Unix *cd* (change directory) command to take you to the Unix directory where your alert log is located:

```
alias log='cd $DBA/$ORACLE_SID/bdump'
```

While aliases are great for saving typing, they are also useful for overriding dangerous Unix defaults. For example, using the Unix *rm* command is very dangerous, because by default it does not ask "are you sure?" before removing files. Using an alias, you can override the default *rm* command to make it ask for confirmation:

```
alias rm='rm -i'
```

Here is a common set of aliases that I use for my Oracle users. I put these in each Oracle user's *.profile* file, and the aliases are automatically available to them every time they sign on to the server:

```
# Aliases
#
alias alert='tail -100\
 $DBA/$ORACLE_SID/bdump/alert_$ORACLE_SID.log|more'
alias arch='cd $DBA/$ORACLE_SID/arch'
alias bdump='cd $DBA/$ORACLE_SID/bdump'
alias cdump='cd $DBA/$ORACLE_SID/cdump'
alias pfile='cd $DBA/$ORACLE_SID/pfile'
alias rm='rm -i'
alias sid='env|grep ORACLE_SID'
alias admin='cd $DBA/admin'
```

The following example shows how aliases such as these can be used in place of typing a long command:

```
corphp*PROD-/home/oracle
>pfile

corphp*PROD-/u01/app/oracle/PROD/pfile
>
```

Notice from the change in the command prompt that the *pfile* alias caused the appropriate *cd* command to be executed.

Any alias can be removed easily with the Unix *unalias* command. For example, to remove the *pfile* alias, you would enter the command *unalias pfile*.

Place a SQL*Plus Script in a Unix Shell Wrapper

Beginners in Unix often find it convenient to execute SQL commands directly from the Unix prompt, without having to enter SQL*Plus each time. The following script shows you how to create a Unix shell wrapper for any set of SQL*Plus commands. The Unix script in this example is named *run_sql.ksh*, and it invokes SQL*Plus to execute a SELECT statement followed by the SQL*Plus script contained in the file */home/oracle/sql/longscript.sql*:

```
>cat run_sql.ksh

#!/bin/ksh

# First, we must set the environment . . . .
ORACLE_SID=mysid
export ORACLE_SID
ORACLE_HOME=\
`cat /etc/oratab|grep ^$ORACLE_SID:|cut -f2 -d':'`
export ORACLE_HOME
PATH=$ORACLE_HOME/bin:$PATH
export PATH

$ORACLE_HOME/bin/sqlplus system/passwd<<!

SELECT * FROM v\$database;
@/home/oracle/sql/longscript.sql

exit
!
```

Note that you can also execute a script directly from the command line, provided that you already have set *ORACLE_HOME* and *ORACLE_SID* in your Unix environment. For example:

```
corphp*PROD-/home/oracle
>sqlplus system/manager @longscript
```

Submit a Task to Run in the Background

The *nohup* command can be used to submit a task as a background process. This is useful for long-running Oracle jobs, because it frees up your command prompt so that you can do other work. It is especially useful when you are dialed in to an Oracle server using a modem, and you want to free up your terminal session.

Assume that you have a script named *run_sql.ksh* that executes SQL*Plus commands. The following *nohup* command can be used to submit that script for background processing:

```
nohup run_sql.ksh > logfile.lst 2>&1 &
```

There's obviously more to this command than just *nohup*, and it's important to understand just what each element of the command is doing. For this example, the elements are as follows:

nohup
> Submits the task so that it continues to run even after you disconnect your terminal session.

run_sql.ksh
> Specifies the Unix shell script that you want to run in the background.

> logfile.lst
> Redirects standard output to the specified file.

2>&1
> Redirects standard error messages to the standard output device. The 2 represents the standard error device, and 1 represents the standard output device.

& Runs the task in the background.

You need to have a space in front of the trailing ampersand (&) character, and it's that & that causes the task to run as a background task. The *nohup* command is frequently used with background tasks, because without it all your background tasks would terminate the moment you logged off of Unix. The *nohup* command allows a task to continue running long after you've logged off and gone home for the night.

Watch the Execution of a Background Process

If you've redirected the output of a background job to a file, you can monitor the execution of that background process by using the *tail –f* command. For example:

```
tail -f logfile.lst
```

The *tail –f* command continuously displays new lines as they are written to the output file, allowing you to easily watch the progress of your background task. To exit the *tail –f* command, enter Ctrl-C at any time.

Ensure That Proper Parameters Are Passed to an Oracle Shell Script

The following code snippet shows how to end a Unix script if appropriate arguments have not been passed to that script. You can use this technique to prevent accidental damage caused by running a critical script without the required inputs.

In this example, the *check_parms.ksh* script requires two parameters: an Oracle SID and a numeric value that must be greater than 100. The *if* statements cause the script to terminate if the required parameters are not passed.

```
# Exit if no first parameter $1.
if [ -z "$1" ]
then
    echo "Usage: check_parms.ksh <ORACLE_SID>\
  <#_days> (where value is > 100)"
    exit 99
fi
```

```
# Exit if no second parameter $2.
if [ -z "$2" ]
then
   echo "Usage: check_parms.ksh <ORACLE_SID>\
 <#_days> (where value is > 100)"
   exit 99
fi

# Exit if parm is not greater than 100.
tmp=`expr $2`      # Convert string to number.
if [ $tmp -lt 101 ]
then
   echo
   echo "Argument two is less than 100.\
 Aborting Script."
   echo
   exit 99
fi
```

In this script, $1 and $2 represent the first and second parameters passed to the script. The −z used in the *if* statements allows you to test for a null parameter value. The first two *if* statements check to see if the required parameters were actually passed. The third *if* statement validates the second parameter to be sure that it is greater than 100.

Ensure That Only the Oracle User Can Run a Script

The following *if* statement will ensure that a Unix script is executed only by the Unix user named *oracle*:

```
if [ `whoami` != 'oracle' ]
then
   echo "Error: You must be oracle to execute."
   exit 99
fi
```

This statement offers extra security and protection against unauthorized execution. For example, a script that shuts down the Oracle database should be executed only by the

---

Oracle user. While Unix permissions offer execution protection, good Unix programmers will also ensure that the proper user is running the script.

Validate an Oracle SID Passed to a Unix Script

The following script shows how to check an Oracle SID to be sure that it's valid. The script expects the SID to be passed in as the first parameter, and it begins by checking to see if a parameter was even passed. The script next counts the number of times the first parameter value appears in the /etc/oratab file. A valid Oracle SID will appear once in that file.

```ksh
#!/bin/ksh

# Exit if no first parameter $1 passed.
if [ -z "$1" ]
then
   echo "Please pass a valid ORACLE_SID\
 to this script"
   exit 99
fi

# Validate the Oracle database name with
# lookup in /etc/oratab.
TEMP=`cat /etc/oratab|grep \^$1:|\
cut -f1 -d':'|wc -l`
tmp=`expr TEMP`     # Convert string to number.
if [ $tmp -ne 1 ]
then
   echo "Your input $1 is not a valid ORACLE_SID."
   exit 99
fi
```

This script fragment is useful when you want to ensure that a valid Oracle SID is passed to a Unix script. Note that if you are using Solaris, the location of the oratab file may be /var/opt/oratab.

Loop Between Unix Servers

The Unix *for* loop construct can be used to loop through all entries in a file on the server. For example, you can write a Unix script that will read all of the entries in your *oratab* file, and visit each of the databases defined in that file. To take this concept further, a Unix script can be made to loop through a file listing all of your server names, causing the Unix script to visit each server.

Combining these two concepts, a single Unix script can loop, server by server, and database by database, to visit each database in your enterprise. This technique is especially useful when all Unix servers are "trusted," meaning that they allow remote shell commands. A remote shell command is a normal Unix command that you submit to run on a remote server. The Unix *rsh* command is used to submit remote shell commands. The *rsh* command is implemented by making an entry in the *.rhosts* file for your Unix Oracle user, authorizing it to connect to the remote host.

For example, if you wish for your Unix Oracle user to be able to connect to the remote server named *prodwest*, then the *prodwest* server must contain an *.rhosts* file in its Oracle user's home directory. This file must contain an entry allowing the remote Oracle user to connect. Your system administrator can help you configure your *.rhosts* file.

The following pseudocode illustrates a double loop. It loops from server to server, and for each server it loops from database to database.

```
FOR every server defined in .rhosts
    FOR every database defined in
        the server's /etc/oratab
            Display $ORACLE_SID
    END
END
```

Here is the actual Unix script that you can use to implement this loop:

```
# Loop through each host name . . .
for host in `cat ~oracle/.rhosts|\
cut -d"." -f1|awk '{print $1}'|sort -u`
do
  echo " "
  echo "************************"
  echo "$host"
  echo "************************"
  # Loop through each database name
  #    /etc/oratab (AIX & HP-UX) or
  #    /var/opt/oracle/oratab in Solaris.
  for db in `rsh $host\
  "cat /etc/oratab|egrep ':N|:Y'|\
grep -v \*|cut -f1 -d':'"`
  do
     # Get the ORACLE_HOME for each database.
     home=`rsh $host "cat /etc/oratab|\
egrep ':N|:Y'|grep -v \*|grep ${db}|\
cut -f2 -d':'"`
     echo " "
     echo "database is $db"
  done
done
```

This particular script does nothing more than use an *echo* command to display each Oracle SID from all the *oratab* files. However, you could easily extend it by adding a *sqlplus* command to invoke a script against each of those SIDs.

Execute a SQL*Plus Script
on All Databases

By expanding on the previous script, you can run a
SQL*Plus script on every database on every one of your
servers. In the following example, a SQL*Plus script is used
to display the optimizer mode setting for every database:

```
# Loop through each host name . . .
for host in `cat ~oracle/.rhosts|\
cut -d"." -f1|awk '{print $1}'|sort -u`
do
    echo " "
    echo "************************"
    echo "$host"
    echo "************************"
    # Loop from database to database.
    for db in `cat /etc/oratab|egrep ':N|:Y'|\
grep -v \*|grep ${db}|cut -f1 -d':'"`
    do
        home=`rsh $host "cat /etc/oratab|egrep\
 ':N|:Y'|grep -v \*|grep ${db}|cut -f2 -d':'"`
        echo "************************"
        echo "database is $db"
        echo "************************"
        rsh $host "
        ORACLE_SID=${db}; export ORACLE_SID;
        ORACLE_HOME=${home}; export ORACLE_HOME;
        ${home}/bin/sqlplus -s /<<!
        set pages 9999;
        set heading off;
        select value from v"\\""$"parameter
        where name='optimizer_mode';
        exit
        !"
    done
done
```

Send Unix Files via Internet Mail

A very handy Unix command will route Unix messages to an Internet-based email address. This command is especially useful for routing Oracle alerts and reports to your email inbox.

The command in the following example emails the contents of the Oracle user's *.sh_history* file. This file contains a record of all Unix commands issued by that user. The subject line on the email will be "Secret DBA Activity Report":

```
cat ~oracle/.sh_history|mailx -s "Secret DBA
Activity Report" donald.burleson@remote-dba.net
```

The *cat* command displays the contents of the file. That output is then piped as input into the *mailx* command. The *mailx* command then emails that input to the specified address.

Change a String in All Files in a Directory

The script shown in this section does a search and replace in all files in a directory, replacing one string with another and making a backup of the original files. The *for* loop that you see in the script causes the *sed* command to be executed for each file in the current directory. The *sed* command does the actual search and replace work, and at the same time it writes the new versions of any affected files to a temporary directory.

```
>cat chg_all.sh

#!/bin/ksh
```

```
tmpdir=tmp.$$

mkdir $tmpdir.new

for f in $*
do
  sed -e 's/oldstring/newstring/g'\
 < $f > $tmpdir.new/$f
done

# Make a backup first!
mkdir $tmpdir.old
mv $* $tmpdir.old/


cd $tmpdir.new
mv $* ../

cd ..
rmdir $tmpdir.new
```

When executing this script, pass in a file mask as an argument. For example, to change only SQL files, the command would be executed like this:

```
root>chg_all.sh *.sql
```

The command in this example causes the string *oldstring* to be changed to *newstring* in all *.sql* files in the current working directory. Remember that the strings to be changed are specified in the script, while the file mask is passed as a parameter. I don't pass the old and new strings as parameters because the *sed* command can be quite tricky, especially if your strings contain special characters.

The *sed* command that you see in the script invokes the "string editor" for Unix. The *sed* command always makes a copy of the changed files, and it never changes a file in-place. Hence, you see in this example that the *sed* command writes new versions of all changed files to the

$tmpdir.new directory. The changes are actually made using *sed* before the backup copies are made. However, the new versions of the files are not copied back from *$tmpdir.new* until after the old versions have been copied to the backup directory.

For more information on using *sed*, refer to the book *sed & awk*, by Dale Dougherty and Arnold Robbins (O'Reilly).

Process Management

This section is designed to provide a basic overview of how you manage Oracle processes in a Unix environment. As you know, an Oracle instance is composed in part of a set of processes such as PMON, SMON, and DBWR. In addition, there are other Unix processes that you need to be aware of and manage. For example, if you are using a dedicated listener (as opposed to the multithreaded server, MTS), then each connected user will have a Unix process.

TIP

Many DBAs call a standard listener a "dedicated" listener because it spawns a dedicated Unix process that connects to Oracle. The MTS does not create a PID for each Oracle connection; instead, it routes the connections through a multi-threaded dispatcher.

This section shows you how to find Oracle processes and identify the ones consuming the most CPU resources. You'll also see how options can be added to the *ps –ef* command to filter and sort the process list output.

Display Unix Processes

The basic process management command is the *ps* command. It is commonly used to display active processes and their characteristics, and displays the values shown in the following example:

```
>ps -ef|grep ora

UID     PID    PPID  C  STIME     TTY  TIME  CMD
oracle 13168    1    0  05:33:06   -   3:15  oracleprod
oracle 26164    1    0  12:57:10   -   4:54  oracleprod
...
```

The column definitions that you should be aware of are as follows:

UID
  The user ID that owns the process.

PID
  The process ID for the task.

PPID
  The parent process. If the parent is 1, the process was created by the *init* process.

STIME
  The start time of the process.

TIME
  The amount of CPU time used by the process so far. This value will increase until the process is complete.

CMD
  The Unix command that is being executed.

The next four sections show several very useful process-management commands that are based on *ps*.

Display Top CPU Consumers

The *ps* command shown in the following example can be used to display the top CPU consumers on a server:

```
>ps -ef|sort +6|tail

oracle 55676    1    0  03:06:16  -  0:36  oracleprod
oracle 24876    1    0  02:52:56  -  0:40  oracleprod
```

```
oracle 41616    1   0 07:00:59   -   0:44 oracleprod
oracle 43460    1   0 02:45:05   -   0:53 oracleprod
oracle 25754    1   0 08:10:03   -   1:01 oracleprod
oracle 17402    1   0 07:27:04   -   2:06 oracleprod
oracle 14922    1   0 01:01:46   -   2:54 oracleprod
oracle 13168    1   0 05:33:06   -   3:15 oracleprod
oracle 26164    1   0 12:57:10   -   4:54 oracleprod
```

Piping the output through the *sort +6* command causes the output of *ps* to be sorted on the sixth column—the amount of CPU time used. Columns are counted from left to right, with the first column being column 0. Since the Unix *sort* command sorts in ascending order (the default for the *sort* command), those processes consuming the most CPU will be at the end of the sorted list. The *sort* output, therefore, is piped to *tail* so that you see only the processes with the highest CPU consumption.

In cases where a process has been running for more than one day, the STIME display format changes from showing the time (08:10:03) to showing the day (Nov 21). The resulting space between the month and the day—for example, between "Nov" and "21"—makes them two distinct columns. Hence, column 7 is now the CPU column:

```
>ps -ef|sort +7|tail
```

```
root  5440  2094 0   Nov 21 -   0:47 /usr/sbin/sysl
root  9244     1 0   Nov 21 -   3:26 ./pdimapsvr.ip
root 10782     1 0   Nov 21 -   4:41 ./pdiconsvr.ip
root  5990  2094 0   Nov 21 -   5:33 /usr/sbin/snmpd
root  4312     1 0   Nov 21 -   7:14 /usr/sbin/cron
root  4448  2094 0   Nov 21 -   9:25 /usr/sbin/rwhod
root     1     0 0   Nov 21 - 198:59 /etc/init
root  2450     1 0   Nov 21 - 438:30 /usr/sbin/syn
```

This column shift from 6 to 7 is a very aggravating problem in Unix, and there is no easy alternative to performing the command twice: once for the current day and again for prior days.

Another approach to finding the top CPU consumers is to use the Berkeley *ps auxgw* command. The third column of the listing produced by *ps auxgw* is named %CPU, and shows the percentage of CPU *currently* being used by each process. You can sort on that column to get a list of the current top CPU users. For example:

```
>ps auxgw|sort +2|tail

oracle   14922   1.0 ... 01:01:46   2:57 oracleprod
oracle   22424   1.0 ... 07:48:43   0:21 oracleprod
oracle   44518   1.0 ... 08:47:47   0:02 oracleprod
oracle   20666   1.6 ... 08:15:19   0:22 oracleprod
oracle   13168   2.4 ... 05:33:06   3:15 oracleprod
oracle   17402   2.4 ... 07:27:04   2:06 oracleprod
oracle   25754   2.7 ... 08:10:03   1:03 oracleprod
oracle   41616   4.4 ... 07:00:59   4:57 oracleprod
```

The difference between these two approaches is that the first looks at overall CPU time used, while the second looks at current CPU utilization.

In yet one more approach, you can use the *egrep* command to filter the output of *ps* in order to display the top CPU consumers. The command *egrep* is an acronym for *extended generalized regular expression parser*. In the following example, the *egrep* command acts as a sort filter for the *ps* command:

```
>ps auxgw|egrep "RSS| "|head

USER      PID  %CPU  %MEM    SZ    RSS TTY       TIME
root      516  78.9   1.0    16      4 - A      Nov 21
oracle  41616   4.4   1.0  8312   6052 - A    07:00:59
oracle  20740   2.7   1.0  8140   5888 - A    08:52:32
oracle  17402   2.4   1.0  8296   6044 - A    07:27:04
oracle  25754   2.4   1.0  8640   6388 - A    08:10:03
oracle  13168   1.6   1.0  8196   5760 - A    05:33:06
oracle  20666   1.0   1.0  8304   6052 - A    08:15:19
oracle  14922   0.6   1.0  8300   5720 - A    01:01:46
oracle  44518   0.6   1.0  8080   5828 - A    08:47:47
```

Show Number of Active Oracle Dedicated Connection Users

It's possible to use *ps* as the basis for a command to count the number of Oracle users in a dedicated server environment. In such an environment, each connected Oracle user will have a corresponding Unix process. The following command can be used to count those processes:

```
ps -ef|grep $ORACLE_SID|grep -v grep|grep -v
ora_|wc -l
```

This command has the following parts:

ps –ef
  Displays all processes

grep $ORACLE_SID
  Filters for processes that represent connections to the specified instance

grep –v grep
  Removes the *grep* command from the result set

*grep –v ora_*
  Removes all Oracle background processes, leaving only the dedicated server processes

wc –l
  Counts the number of lines, which corresponds to the number of remaining processes, and therefore to the number of connections

Here's an example of this command being used. Note that the output is just a single number:

```
>ps -ef|grep $ORACLE_SID|grep -v grep|grep -v ora_|wc -l

        23
```

As you can see in this example, there are 23 users connected to the Oracle instance specified by *$ORACLE_SID*.

Kill Processes

There are times when it is necessary to kill all Oracle processes or a selected set of Oracle processes. You will want
to kill all Oracle processes when the database is "locked,"
and you cannot enter Server Manager or SQL*Plus. The *kill*
command can be used for this purpose. Note that when
you kill Oracle background processes such as PMON and
SMON, you must also issue the *ipcs* command to ensure
that all memory segments used by those processes are
removed. The *ipcs* command is discussed in detail later in
this book.

The basic format of the *kill* command is:

```
kill -9 PID1 PID2 PID3...
```

To kill all Oracle processes (for all instances), you can issue
the following command:

```
ps -ef|grep "ora_"|grep -v grep|awk '{print $2}'|xargs
-i kill -9 {}
```

There are times when even the *kill –9* command fails to
remove a process. This problem can be overcome by piping */dev/null* to the ttyname as a part of the *kill* command.
The following is the command to use, and it's indispens-
able for killing stubborn tasks:

```
cat /dev/null > /dev/your_ttyname kill -9 PID#
```

You can get the value for *your_ttyname* from the output of
the *ps –ef* command. Look under the TTY column.

Pin the Oracle SGA in Memory

In HP-UX, Solaris, and some other SVR4 versions of Unix, it is possible to "pin" the Oracle SGA in memory so that it will never experience a page-in. A *page-in* occurs whenever part of the SGA is swapped out to disk and then read back again. You cannot do this on AIX. Depending on your operating system, the pinning is done by setting one of the following *INIT.ORA* parameters:

```
# For HP-UX, use lock_sga:
LOCK_SGA=true

# For Sun Solaris, use USE_ISM.
# ISM is an acronym for "Intimate
# Shared Memory".
USE_ISM=true
```

TIP

In Oracle 8.1.5 and above, *USE_ISM* is a hidden parameter, and it defaults to true. A hidden parameter is one that is not listed in the Oracle documentation, but that still exists for use by Oracle Support Services.

Server Values

Unix has a wealth of system configuration values that you can look at. These include kernel parameters as well as server device values that tell you about devices, such as memory and disk drives, that are installed on your server. Kernel parameters affect Unix's operation at a very fundamental level, and some of them are important to consider when you install Oracle on a Unix server.

This section shows you how to use the *lsdev* command to look at server device values. The *lsdev* command works under both HP-UX and AIX. You'll also learn how to display kernel parameter values. Under HP-UX, the *kmtune* command is used for that purpose. Under AIX, you use *lsattr*.

Display Server Device Values in HP-UX

Using the *lsdev* command, you can display information about all the devices connected to your server. This includes disk drives, memory, CPUs, buses, and other hardware components. In the example that follows, the *lsdev* command is used to list all mounted devices for a server:

```
>lsdev
    Character       Block        Driver        Class
        0            -1          cn            pseudo
        3            -1          mm            pseudo
       16            -1          ptym          ptym
       17            -1          ptys          ptys
       27            -1          dmem          pseudo
       28            -1          diag0         diag
       46            -1          netdiag1      unknown
       52            -1          lan2          lan
```

The Character, Block, and Class columns are not relevant to this discussion. The Driver column is the one you want to look at. It shows a list of device drivers, and hence a list of devices that are attached to the server.

Display Server Device Values in AIX

Just as with HP-UX, the AIX *lsdev* command displays all the devices on the AIX server. However, while the command is the same, the –*C* flag is required under AIX. Also notice

---

that the output is quite different from the *lsdev* command in HP-UX.

```
>lsdev -C

sys0          ...    System Object
sysplanar0    ...    System Planar
pci0          ...    PCI Bus
pci1          ...    PCI Bus
isa0          ...    ISA Bus
sa0           ...    Standard I/O Serial Port
sa1           ...    Standard I/O Serial Port
scsi0         ...    Wide SCSI I/O Controller
hdisk0        ...    16 Bit SCSI Disk Drive
hdisk1        ...    16 Bit SCSI Disk Drive
...
```

Display System Kernel Parameters in HP-UX

You can use the *kmtune* command to display all of the kernel configuration parameter settings for HP-UX Version 11. Certain kernel parameters, such as *semmni* and *maxusers*, are critical to the successful operation of Oracle under Unix. Here's an example showing the type of output that you'll get from *kmtune*:

```
>kmtune

Parameter               Value
===================================================
NSTRBLKSCHED            2
NSTREVENT               50
NSTRPUSH                16
NSTRSCHED               0
STRCTLSZ                1024
STRMSGSZ                65535
acctresume              4
acctsuspend             2
aio_listio_max          256
...
```

```
semmni              200
semmns              800
semmnu              30
semume              10
semvmx              32767
sendfile_max        0
shmem               1
shmmax              1073741824
shmmni              500
shmseg              300
...
```

The *kmtune* command can be refined using *grep* so that it displays only a desired class of values. In the next example, *grep* is added to the *kmtune* command to filter out only those kernel parameters relating to shared memory:

```
>kmtune|grep -i shm

shmem               1
shmmax              1073741824
shmmni              500
shmseg              300
```

Display System Kernel Parameters in AIX

Unlike HP-UX, AIX does not have a *kmtune* command. Instead, in AIX, you use the *lsattr* command to view settings for kernel parameters. For example:

```
>lsattr -El sys0
maxbuf    20 Maximum number of pages in block...
maxmbuf    0 Maximum Kbytes of real memory al...
maxuproc 200 Maximum number of PROCESSES allo...
iostat   true Continuously maintain DISK I/O h...
realmem 3137536 Amount of usable physical mem...
modelname    IBM,9076-WCN  Machine name      ...
systemid     IBM,010013864 Hardware system ide...
...
```

This command is useful for displaying system variables such as *maxuproc* and *maxbuf* that are used by Oracle.

Memory and CPU Management

This section is devoted to the commands that show memory and CPU consumption. As you know, an Oracle database does not exist in a vacuum. If the database server is experiencing a CPU overload or a memory-swapping problem, no amount of Oracle tuning can relieve that. Hence, it is very important that you be able to see when your server is overloaded.

The commands described in this section often differ between Unix dialects. Some dialects, such as Solaris, do not support memory-display commands. In those cases, GUI tools such as *glance* must be used to see memory values.

Display RAM Size in DEC Unix

In DEC Unix, you can use the *uerf* command in conjunction with *grep* to display memory size. For example:

```
uerf -r 300 | grep -i mem
```

Here, the output of the *uerf* command is piped to *grep* to filter out and display the segments relating to memory. The *–i* option causes *grep* to find both uppercase and lowercase strings. With respect to the example shown here, *grep –i mem* looks for both *MEM* and *mem*.

Display RAM Size in HP-UX

In HP-UX, you can run the *glance* or *sar* utilities in order to see the amount of RAM available. The *glance* utility displays a screen showing CPU and memory utilization both for the system as a whole and for individual processes. The *sar* utility displays a complete set of system settings and also shows overall server performance. Because it consists of more than 50 screens, a discussion of *sar* is beyond the scope of this text. For more information on *glance* or *sar*, look to the manpages on your Unix server.

Display RAM Size in Solaris

The *prtconf* command can be used on Solaris servers to quickly see the amount of available memory. For example:

```
>prtconf|grep -i mem

Memory size: 2048 Mbytes
    memory (driver not attached)
    virtual memory (driver not attached)
```

Display RAM Size in AIX

In IBM's AIX dialect of Unix, you can use the *lsdev* command followed by the *lsattr* command to display the amount of memory on a server. First execute *lsdev* to list all devices. Then pipe that output through *grep* to filter out everything not related to memory. That will get you the names of the memory devices that are installed. For example:

```
>lsdev -C|grep mem

mem0       Available 00-00            Memory
```

Here you can see that *mem0* is the name of the memory device. Now that you have the name, you can issue the *lsattr –El* command to see the amount of memory on the server. In the following example, the server has three gigabytes of RAM installed:

```
>lsattr -El mem0

size     3064 Total amount of physical memory in Mbytes
goodsize 3064 Amount of usable physical memory in
Mbytes
```

You must issue the *lsattr —El* command separately for each memory device.

Use svmon in AIX

The IBM AIX dialect of Unix has a server monitor utility called *svmon*. The *svmon* utility displays a usage map of all memory on the server, including memory in use and paging space. For example:

```
root@AIX1 [/]#svmon

             size   inuse free   pin virtual
memory    1048566 1023178 4976 55113  251293
pg space   524288   10871

             work    pers clnt
pin         55116       0    0
in use     250952  772224    2
```

The column descriptions for the *svmon* command's output are as follows:

size

> The number of real memory frames. In Unix, a frame is equivalent to a page, and the page size is 4K bytes.

inuse

> The number of frames containing pages

free

> The amount of memory that is not being used

pin

> The number of frames containing pinned pages in use

virtual

> The amount of virtual memory available

The *svmon* command can also be used with the *—P* option to display characteristics for a specific process. Pass the process ID (PID) as a parameter to the *—P* option. For example:

```
root>svmon -P 26060
```

```
          pid command   inuse      pin     pgsp  virtual
        26060 pr          6871     1607     1022     6001

         vsid     esid type description              inuse
        24029        d work shared library text       3992
            0        0 work kernel seg                 2509
        105e4        2 work process private            188
        285ea        f work shared library data         92
        185e6        1 pers code,/dev/lvs001:301         81
        6c59b        - pers /dev/lvs001:92402             6
        744fd        - pers /dev/lvs001:763909            3
        7c5ff        - pers /dev/lvs001:1327130           0
```

This command is especially useful if you want to see the inner memory usage for a specific Oracle process. For example, if you see an Oracle process that you suspect to be in a loop, use the *svmon –P* command to reveal the actual memory usage for the task. Oracle tasks that are in a memory loop will often use excessive memory.

Display Allocated Memory Segments

To see all allocated memory segments for your server, enter the *ipcs* command as shown in the following example:

```
>ipcs -pmb

IPC status from /dev/mem as of Thu May 11 09:40:59 EDT
2000

T       ID KEY         ... OWNER GROUP     SEGSZ   CPID
Shared Memory:
m     4096 0x670610c5  ... root system        12 45082
m     4097 0x680610c5  ... root system    106496 45082
m     4098 0x78041249  ... root system    777216 47010
m     4099 0x78061865  ... root system      7536 47880
m        4 0x0d05014f  ... root system      1440 16968
m   368645 0x0fe2eb3d  ...oracle  dba    35610624 17760
m   401414 0x0f97693e  ...oracle  dba   229863424 61820
m   274439 0x0fefeae2  ...oracle  dba    35610624 21992
m   184328 0x0fefeb6e  ...oracle  dba    35610624 46690
```

```
m   151561 0x0fe2eb03 ...oracle   dba    4972544 71116
m     8202 0x0f956d88 ...oracle   dba   31117312 72448
m   143371 0x0f96e941 ...oracle   dba   21200896 83662
m   135180 0x78041185 ...  root system     2656 81312
```

The processes owned by the Oracle user are associated
with the Oracle System Global Area (SGA). To see information about the specific memory segments allocated to an
instance, you can enter Server Manager (or SQL*Plus as
SYSDBA in Oracle8*i*), connect to the instance, and issue
the *oradebug ipc* command. For example:

```
SVRMGR>oradebug ipc
-------------- Shared memory --------------
Seg Id      Address   Size
401414      40000000  229863424
Total: # of segments = 1, size = 229863424
-------------- Semaphores ---------------
Total number of semaphores = 200
Number of semaphores per set = 0
Number of semaphore sets = 0
Semaphore identifiers:
```

TIP

Under some operating systems, the *oradebug* output is written to a trace file rather than to a display.

Only one memory segment has been allocated to this
instance. The segment ID (from the Seg Id column) is
401414. That corresponds to the ID column in the *ipcs*
command output. The size of the segment, 229,863,424 in
this case, represents the size of the SGA.

Manually Deallocate a Memory Segment

When an Oracle instance crashes, sometimes its memory
segments are still held as allocated by the server. When this
happens, they must be manually deallocated. One way to

---

do this is to use the *ipcrm* command, passing in the segment ID as an argument. You can get the segment ID from the *ipcs* command output. For example, the following command deallocates segment ID 401414:

```
ipcrm -m 401414
```

WARNING

Be very careful with the *ipcrm* command! You can easily clobber the SGA for a running instance. Only use this command when the background processes for an instance have abnormally died.

Display the Number of CPUs

The *lsdev* command can be used to see the number of CPUs on a server. This is very important, because it shows the number of parallel query processes that can be used on that server. That in turn limits the value that you can use following the DEGREE keyword in a parallel query or DML statement. The following example is taken from an AIX server and shows that the server has four CPUs:

```
>lsdev -C|grep Process|wc -l
```

```
    4
```

The key is to pipe the output of *lsdev* through *grep*, filter out just those lines containing the string "Process" (those refer to CPUs), and then pipe those lines through *wc* to get a count.

Display the number of CPUs in Solaris

In Solaris, the *prsinfo* command can be used to count the number of CPUs on the server. For example:

```
>psrinfo -v|grep "Status of processor"|wc -l
```

```
    2
```

To see details about the CPUs, you can use the −*v* (verbose) option:

```
>psrinfo -v
```

```
Status of processor 0 as of: 12/13/00 14:47:41
   Processor has been on-line since 11/05/00 13:26:42.
   The sparcv9 processor operates at 450 MHz, and has a
        sparcv9 floating-point processor.
Status of processor 2 as of: 12/13/00 14:47:41
   Processor has been on-line since 11/05/00 13:26:43.
   The sparcv9 processor operates at 450 MHz, and has a
        sparcv9 floating-point processor.
```

Semaphore Management

Semaphores are signals used by Oracle to serialize the internal Oracle processes. The number of semaphores for a database is equal to the value of the *PROCESSES* parameter in the *INIT.ORA* file. For example, a database with *PROCESSES=200* will have 200 semaphores allocated for Oracle.

TIP

AIX Unix does not use semaphores. In AIX, the post/wait driver is used instead, because it increases performance.

It is critical that the Unix kernel parameter *semmns* be set to at least double the total number of processes for all database instances on your server. If it's not set, your databases will fail to start, and you'll receive the following error:

```
spcre: semget error, unable to get first semaphore set.
```

Change Kernel Parameters

It's often necessary to make changes to kernel parameters on a Unix system in order to accommodate the needs of the Oracle database software. You should always work with

---

your Unix system administrator to make such changes. The general process, however, is as follows:

1. Shut down any running Oracle instances.

2. Locate the kernel configuration file for your operating system.

3. Make the necessary changes using system utilities or the *vi* editor. System utilities for several common Unix variants are listed in Table 1-1.

4. Reconfigure the kernel.

5. Reboot your machine.

6. Restart your Oracle instances.

Remember, kernel configuration requires a great deal of expertise. Always work with your system administrator.

Table 1-1. Utilities to Change Kernel Parameters

Operating System	Utility
HP-UX	*SAM*
SCO	*SYSADMSH*
AIX	*SMIT*
Solaris	*ADMINTOOL*

WARNING

Reconfiguring kernel parameters can have a dramatic impact on your server. The effects of a mistake can be catastrophic. Hence, you need to make sure that you fully understand kernel configuration before attempting any such changes.

Display Values for Semaphores

The maximum allowed number of semaphores is specified by the *semmns* kernel parameter. In HP-UX Version 11, the command to show semaphores is *kmtune*. Run *kmtune*,

---

and pipe the output through *grep sem* to filter out everything except semaphore settings. For example:

```
>kmtune|grep sem
sema         1
semaem       16384
semmap       (SEMMNI+2)
semmni       200
semmns       800
semmnu       30
semume       10
semvmx       32767
```

Look at this output, find the line for *semmns*, and you'll quickly see that the server has 800 semaphores.

Count Used Semaphores

You can use the *–sa* option of the *ipcs* command to display the number of used semaphores. The total number of used semaphores is determined by summing the NSEMS column, which is the far right column in the output. For example:

```
>ipcs -sa|grep oracle

s  221 0x0000 --ra-r-----  oracle  dba   200
s  223 0x0000 --ra-r-----  oracle  dba   200
s 1024 0x0000 --ra-r-----  oracle  dba   100
s  225 0x0000 --ra-r-----  oracle  dba    75
```

From this output, you can determine the following:

- There are four instances running—one for each line of output.
- There are 575 (200+200+100+75) semaphores held by the Oracle user for those four database instances.

The output from the *ipcs –sa* command will always display one line per instance. From there, it's just a matter of summing the rightmost column to get the total number of semaphores that are being used.

Determine the Semaphore Sets Held by an Instance

When you need to remove a semaphore set for a crashed instance, you cannot tell using the *ipcs −sa* command just which semaphore sets are associated with which instances. You can, however, get this information by using Server Manager's *oradebug* command. Here's an example:

```
>svrmgrl

Oracle Server Manager Release 3.0.5.0.0 - Production

(c) Copyright 1997, Oracle Corporation.  All Rights
Reserved.

Oracle8 Enterprise Edition Release 8.0.5.1.0 -
Production
PL/SQL Release 8.0.5.1.0 - Production

SVRMGR>connect internal;

Connected.

SVRMGR>oradebug ipc

Shared memory information written to trace file.
```

Server Manager writes *oradebug* output to a trace file; look in your *udump* directory for a *.trc* file. The contents will appear as follows:

```
------------------ Semaphores ------------------
Total number of semaphores = 100
Number of semaphores per set = 100
Number of semaphore sets = 1
Semaphore identifiers:
 14825
```

The IDs of the semaphore sets used by the instance are listed under the "Semaphore identifiers" heading. In this case, the instance is using just one semaphore set: ID 14825.

Remove a Held Semaphore After a Crash

When an Oracle instance crashes, background processes are killed, but the memory for the SGA region is sometimes still held by the server. The *ipcs* command in the following example will identify those semaphores that are being used by Oracle instances:

```
>ipcs -sa|grep oracle

s  221 0x0000 --ra-r-----   oracle   dba   200
s  223 0x0000 --ra-r-----   oracle   dba   200
s 1024 0x0000 --ra-r-----   oracle   dba   100
s  225 0x0000 --ra-r-----   oracle   dba    75
```

Now you have to determine which semaphore set is associated with the crashed instance—you do not want to delete the wrong set. If you have only one instance on your server, you'll have only one Oracle semaphore set to choose from. If you have multiple instances, use the *oradebug* command described earlier to determine the semaphore sets used by each of the *surviving* instances. Then, through the process of elimination, you can determine the set associated with the crashed instance.

TIP

The *PROCESSES* parameter in your instance's *INIT.ORA* parameter file usually matches the number of semaphores for the instance. You can sometimes use this parameter to determine which set of semaphores to delete.

Once you identify the sets of semaphores that you wish to release, you can issue the *ipcrm −s* command to release them. The following example releases semaphore sets 221 and 223:

```
>ipcrm -s 221
>ipcrm -s 223
>
>ipcs -sa|grep oracle
```

```
s  1024 0x0000 --ra-r-----    oracle    dba    100
s   225 0x0000 --ra-r-----    oracle    dba     75
```

System Log Messages

The commands described in this section are used to display the OS error logs. These logs can be useful for detecting transient disk I/O problems, memory failures, and other such problems.

Because each dialect of Unix was created differently, the system logs are in different locations, and different commands are used to display the messages.

Show Server Log in HP-UX

Unix server log messages in HP-UX are kept in the */var/adm/syslog/syslog.log* file. This file will display messages relating to any server-related problems with disk I/O, memory, or CPU. This is one of the first places to look when an Oracle database has crashed, because you must first rule out server problems before attempting to fix the database.

The following example shows the *grep* command being used to display lines from the server log that contain the text "error":

```
>grep error /var/adm/syslog/syslog.log|more

May  1 20:30:08 sprihp01 syslog: NetWorker media:
(warning) /dev/rmt/c5t6d0BESTn reading: I/O error
```

Show Server Log in AIX

In AIX, you do not need to know the file location for the system log. Issuing the *errpt* command will display the error log, which shows any server-related errors. For example:

```
>errpt -a|more
```

```
LABEL:          CORE_DUMP
IDENTIFIER:     C60BB505

Date/Time:      Tue May  9 10:34:47
Sequence Number: 24908
Machine Id:     000138644C00
Node Id:        sp2k6n03
Class:          S
Type:           PERM
Resource Name:  SYSPROC
```

Server Monitoring

It is critical to check your server whenever you see a performance problem. You must rule out the server as the source of a performance problem before attempting to do any Oracle tuning. The only effective way to monitor the complete behavior of an Oracle database is to monitor both the database server and the database itself.

There is a host of Unix commands that display CPU and memory consumption. Common utilities include *top*, *sar*, and *vmstat*.

Use top

Use the *top* utility to show the top sessions on a Unix server. The *top* command shows the relative activity for each CPU in the CPU cluster. The output from *top* is in two sections. The first section shows the load on each processor, while the second section lists the current top sessions in terms of CPU utilization. The following example shows the first section of *top* output:

```
Server1>top

System: corp-hp9 Thu Jul  6 09:14:23 2000
Load averages: 0.04, 0.03, 0.03
340 processes: 336 sleeping, 4 running
CPU states:
CPU   LOAD   USER   NICE   SYS   IDLE...
```

```
0    0.06    5.0%    0.0%    0.6%   94.4%...
1    0.06    0.0%    0.0%    0.8%   99.2%...
2    0.06    0.8%    0.0%    0.0%   99.2%...
3    0.06    0.0%    0.0%    0.2%   99.8%...
4    0.00    0.0%    0.0%    0.0%  100.0%...
5    0.00    0.2%    0.0%    0.0%   99.8%...
---  ----   -----   -----   -----  -----...
avg  0.04    1.0%    0.0%    0.2%   98.8%...

...  BLOCK   SWAIT   INTR   SSYS
...  0.0%    0.0%    0.0%   0.0%
...  0.0%    0.0%    0.0%   0.0%
...  0.0%    0.0%    0.0%   0.0%
...  0.0%    0.0%    0.0%   0.0%
...  0.0%    0.0%    0.0%   0.0%
...  0.0%    0.0%    0.0%   0.0%
...  -----   -----   -----  -----
...  0.0%    0.0%    0.0%   0.0%
```

At the very beginning of this section, before the tabular output begins, you see three values for the load average. The *load average* is an arbitrary number that describes the load on the system. The first load average value is the immediate load for the past minute. The next value represents the load average for the past 5 minutes. The third value is the load average for the past 15 minutes.

The second section of *top* output, which details the current top sessions in terms of CPU utilization, appears as follows:

```
Memory: 493412K (229956K) real, 504048K (253952K)
virtual, 767868K free  Page# 1/49

CPU TTY  PID USERNAME PRI NI   SIZE    RES...
 0   ? 26835 applmgr  154 20 30948K 11936K...
 2   ? 27210 applmgr  154 20 31316K 12836K...
 5   ?    36 root     152 20    0K    0K...
 1   ?   347 root     154 20   32K   96K...
 5   ? 27429 oracle   154 20 20736K  2608K...
 4   ? 27067 oracle   154 20 21984K  3792K...

...  STATE   TIME %WCPU
```

```
...    sleep     0:49   3.91
...    sleep     0:49   1.91
...    run      56:28   1.16
...    sleep   567:15   1.11
...    sleep     0:23   0.39
...    sleep     1:31   0.36
```

The second part of the *top* output shows the top sessions.
You see the process ID (PID), the username, the dispatching priority (PRI), the nice value (NI), the size of each task's
memory (SIZE), the state, the execution time, and the percentage of CPU being used by each process.

While *top* has many columns of information, there are only
a few that are of interest to you as a DBA:

Load averages
> These are the load averages for the entire server. Values
> greater than 1 may indicate an overload problem on the
> server.

CPU
> The first section of the *top* output shows a load summary
> for each CPU. The CPU column in the detailed listing
> shows which CPU is servicing each individual task.

LOAD
> The LOAD column shows the load on each of the CPUs.

IDLE
> The IDLE column shows the percentage of time that
> each CPU has been idle.

Use sar

The *sar* utility (System Activity Reporter) is quite popular in
SVR4 environments such as HP-UX and Solaris. It is also
becoming widely available for AIX.

Just like *top*, *sar* gives detailed information about Oracle
tasks from the Unix level. You will be able to see the overall consumption of CPU, disk, memory, and Journal File
System (JFS) buffer usage.

There are three major flags that you can use with *sar*:

sar −*u*

  Shows CPU activity

sar −*w*

  Shows swapping activity

sar −*b*

  Shows buffer activity

TIP

Each flavor of Unix has a different implementation of *sar*. For example, some of the key flags used in the Solaris version of *sar* are not available in HP-UX. The examples in this book show the HP-UX version of *sar*.

The output from a *sar* report usually shows a time-based snapshot of activity. This is true for all reports that you'll see in this section. When you issue the *sar* command, you pass two numeric arguments. The first represents the time interval between samples and the second represents the number of samples to take. For example:

```
sar -u 10 5
```

The *sar* command in this example is requesting five samples taken at 10-second intervals.

sar −u (CPU report)

The *sar* −*u* command is very useful for seeing the overall CPU consumption over time. CPU time can be allocated into the following four buckets: user mode, system mode, waiting on I/O, and idle. In the example that follows, I execute *sar* −*u* to see the state of the CPU:

```
ROOT>sar -u 2 5

HP-UX burleson B.11.00 U 9000/800      08/09/00
```

08:37:06	%usr	%sys	%wio	%idle
08:37:06	43	57	0	0
08:37:08	45	55	0	0
08:37:10	44	56	0	0
08:37:12	44	56	0	0
08:37:14	43	57	0	0

sar –w (memory switching and swapping activity)

The *sar–w* command is especially useful if you suspect that your database server is experiencing a memory shortage. When an Oracle server runs short of real memory, segments of RAM are swapped out to a swap disk. Such page-out operations happen frequently, but a page-in indicates that the Oracle server is exceeding the amount of RAM. The usual remedies for swapping are to reduce the size of the SGA and/or to buy more RAM for the database server.

The following example shows the swapping activity report that you get from *sar*:

```
ROOT>sar -w 5 5

HP-UX corp-hp1 B.11.00 U 9000/800    08/09/00

19:37:57 swpin/s bswin/s swpot/s bswot/s pswch/s
19:38:02   0.00     0.0    0.00     0.0     222
19:38:07   0.00     0.0    0.00     0.0     314
19:38:12   0.00     0.0    0.00     0.0     280
19:38:17   0.00     0.0    0.00     0.0     295
19:38:22   0.00     0.0    0.00     0.0     359

Average    0.00     0.0    0.00     0.0     294
```

The columns have the following meanings:

swpin/s
> Number of process swap-ins per second

swpot/s
> Number of process swap-outs per second

---

bswin/s

Number of 512-byte swap-ins per second

bswot/s

Number of 512-byte swap-outs per second

pswch/s

Number of process context switches per second

sar –b (buffer activity report)

The *sar –b* command causes *sar* to report buffer activity, which equates to disk I/O activity and is especially useful if you suspect that your database is I/O-bound. The report shows real disk I/O and the interaction with the Unix Journal File System (JFS) buffer. For example:

```
root>sar -b 1 6

HP-UX corp-hp1 B.11.00 U 9000/800    08/09/00

19:44:53 lread/s %rcache bwrit/s lwrit/s...
19:44:54      91     100       9      19...
19:44:55       0       0       0       5...
19:44:56       6     100       9       8...
19:44:57      30     100       9      20...
19:44:58       1     100       0       3...
19:44:59       1     100       9       4...
Average       22     100       6      10...

%wcache pread/s pwrit/s...
     53       0       0...
    100       0       0...
      0       0       0...
     55       0       0...
    100       0       0...
      0       0       0...
     39       0       0...
```

In the output shown, you see the following columns:

lread/s
> Number of reads per second from the Unix JFS buffer cache

%rcache
> Buffer cache hit ratio (for the Unix JFS buffer cache) for read requests

bwrit/s
> Number of physical writes to disk per second

lwrit/s
> Number of writes per second to the Unix JFS buffer cache

%wcache
> Buffer cache hit ratio (for the Unix JFS buffer cache) for write requests

pread/s
> Number of reads per second from disk

pwrit/s
> Number of writes per second to disk

Use sadc

sadc is an acronym for System Activity Data Collector, a part of the System Activity Report Package. *sadc* is a popular utility that can be used in conjunction with *cron* to schedule the collection of server statistics. All of the *sadc* reports are located in the */usr/lbin/sa* directory. These reports must be run as root, and they provide detailed server information. One of the most popular *sadc* reports is *sa1*.

Unlike the *top* or *glance* reports, *sadc* reports are invoked from a script. In the example that follows, you'll see that the *sal.sh* script invokes *sadc* on your behalf in order to generate the *sa1* report:

```
ROOT>cat /usr/lbin/sa/sa1.sh
```

```
#! /usr/bin/sh
# @(#) $Revision: 1.4 $
#       sa1.sh

DATE=`date +%d`
ENDIR=/usr/lbin/sa
DFILE=/var/adm/sa/sa$DATE
cd $ENDIR
if [ $# = 0 ]
then
        exec $ENDIR/sadc 1 1 $DFILE
else
        exec $ENDIR/sadc $* $DFILE
fi
```

Again, *sadc* is used only in situations where you want to regularly schedule the collection of server statistics using the *cron* utility.

Use vmstat

The *vmstat* utility is the most common Unix monitoring utility, and it is found in the majority of Unix dialects (*vmstat* is called *osview* in IRIX). The *vmstat* utility displays various server values at a given time interval. The first numeric argument to *vmstat* represents the time interval expressed in seconds. In the example that follows, I execute *vmstat 3* and get a line of output every three seconds:

```
>vmstat 3

kthr            memory              cpu
----    ...   ---------------   ...  --------------
r  b    ...   fre  re  pi  sr   ...  cs  us sy id wa
0  0    ...   207   0   1   0   ...  142 18  4 75  4
0  0    ...   187   0   4   0   ...   70  2  1 91  6
0  0    ...   184   0   0   0   ...   99  5  2 89  4
0  0    ...   165   0   0   0   ...   98  1  8 52 40
0  0    ...   150   0   3   0   ...  136  4  2 87  6
0  0    ...   141   0   1   0   ...  192  5  0 91  4
```

You can exit *vmstat* at any time by pressing Ctrl-C.

The critical *vmstat* values that you need to know about are as follows:

r The run queue. When this value exceeds the number of CPUs, the server is experiencing a CPU bottleneck. (You can get the number of CPUs by entering *lsdev –C |grep Process |wc –l.*)

pi The page-in count. Non-zero values typically indicate that the server is short on memory and that RAM is being written to the swap disk. However, non-zero values can also occur when numerous programs are accessing memory for the first time. To find out which is the case, check the scan rate (*sr*) column. If both the page-in count and the scan rate are non-zero, then you are short on RAM.

sr The scan rate. If you see the scan rate rising steadily, you know that the paging daemon is busy allocating memory pages.

For AIX and HP-UX, *vmstat* also provides the following CPU values. These values are expressed as percentages and will sum to 100:

us User CPU percentage

sy System CPU percentage

id Idle CPU percentage

wa Wait CPU percentage

When the sum of user and system CPU percentages (*us+sy*) approaches 100, then the CPUs are busy, but not necessarily overloaded. The run queue value can indicate a CPU overload, but only when the run queue exceeds the number of CPUs on the server.

When wait CPU percentages (the *wa* values) exceed 20, then 20% or more of the processing time is waiting for a resource, usually I/O. It is common to see high wait CPU percentages during backups and exports, but they can also indicate an I/O bottleneck.

Automate vmstat Collection

Now that you understand how to use *vmstat,* you'll find it easy to automate the process and store the *vmstat* information in an Oracle table. This allows you to maintain an historical record of all server activity. The scripts shown in this section automate the collection of *vmstat* statistics over time and were designed for the AIX and HP-UX dialects of Unix. However, they can easily be modified for Solaris users.

TIP

For Solaris users, you need to alter the *get_vmstat.ksh* script to use *vmstat –n.* You also need to account for the changes in column output between the two systems.

---

cr_vmstat_tab.sql

The following script (which you could name *cr_vmstat_ tab.sql*) is a SQL*Plus script to create the table used to record statistics gathered over time. You should modify the storage parameters and tablespace name to suit your environment.

```
DROP TABLE MON_VMSTATS;
CREATE TABLE MON_VMSTATS
(
     START_DATE          DATE,
     DURATION            NUMBER,
     SERVER_NAME         VARCHAR2(20),
     RUNQUE_WAITS        NUMBER,
     PAGE_IN             NUMBER,
     PAGE_OUT            NUMBER,
     USER_CPU            NUMBER,
     SYSTEM_CPU          NUMBER,
     IDLE_CPU            NUMBER,
     WAIT_CPU            NUMBER
)
tablespace dba_perf
```

```
STORAGE (INITIAL 500K
        NEXT   500K
        PCTINCREASE 0)
;
```

get_vmstat.ksh

Following is the *get_vmstat.ksh* script, which uses *vmstat* to gather statistics and then stores them in the *MON_VMSTATS* table. The script is currently set to sample the statistics every five minutes.

```
#!/bin/ksh

# First, we must set the environment.
ORACLE_SID=BURLESON
export ORACLE_SID
ORACLE_HOME=`cat /etc/oratab|\
grep \^$ORACLE_SID:|cut -f2 -d':'`
export ORACLE_HOME
PATH=$ORACLE_HOME/bin:$PATH
export PATH
MON=`echo ~oracle/mon`
export MON

SERVER_NAME=`uname -a|awk '{print $2}'`
typeset -u SERVER_NAME
export SERVER_NAME

# Sample every five minutes (300 seconds).
SAMPLE_TIME=300

while true
do
   vmstat ${SAMPLE_TIME} 2 > /tmp/msg$$

# This script is intended to run starting at
# 7:00 AM EST until midnight EST.
cat /tmp/msg$$|sed 1,4d | awk  '{ \
printf("%s %s %s %s %s %s %s\n", $1, $6, $7,\
 $14, $15, $16, $17) }' | while read RUNQUE\
 PAGE_IN PAGE_OUT USER_CPU SYSTEM_CPU\
```

```
IDLE_CPU WAIT_CPU
    do

        $ORACLE_HOME/bin/sqlplus -s / <<EOF
        insert into mon_vmstats values (
                                sysdate,
                                $SAMPLE_TIME,
                                '$SERVER_NAME',
                                $RUNQUE,
                                $PAGE_IN,
                                $PAGE_OUT,
                                $USER_CPU,
                                $SYSTEM_CPU,
                                $IDLE_CPU,
                                $WAIT_CPU
                                    );
        EXIT
EOF
    done
done


    rm /tmp/msg$$
```

As shown here, the script pulls columns from the *vmstat*
output that are appropriate for an AIX environment.
Table 1-2 shows the column mappings to use in other Unix
environments. These are used in the print statement.

Table 1-2. vmstat Column Mappings

	HP-UX	AIX	Solaris	Linux
Run queue	1	1	1	1
Page-in	8	6	8	8
Page-out	9	7	9	9
User	16	14	20	14
System	17	15	21	15
Idle	18	16	22	16
Wait	n/a	17	n/a	n/a

This script assumes the use of operating-system authentication to log in to your database. If that's not the case in your environment, you can modify the *sqlplus* command to include a username and password on the command line. It's best, though, to avoid including such information in a script.

Sample vmstat report

Once you have captured your statistics into Oracle tables, you can report on them. In the example that follows, you see a SQL*Plus script that computes the average of the sum of the user and system CPU values for your database server. It will compute other averages as well: just uncomment the lines for other values of interest. Using a spreadsheet such as Microsoft Excel, you can chart this data to get a graphical view of CPU utilization.

```
set pages 9999;

set feedback off;
set verify off;

column my_date heading 'date' format a20
column c2        heading runq  format 999
column c3        heading pg_in format 999
column c4        heading pg_ot format 999
column c5        heading usr   format 99
column c6        heading sys   format 99
column c7        heading idl   format 99
column c8        heading wt    format 99


select
 to_char(start_date,'day') my_date,
-- avg(runque_waits)         c2
-- avg(page_in)              c3,
-- avg(page_out)             c4,
avg(user_cpu + system_cpu) c5,
-- avg(system_cpu)           c6,
-- avg(idle_cpu)             c7,
```

```
avg(wait_cpu)              c8
from
mon_vmstats
 group  BY
 to_char(start_date,'day')
;
```

This script will return a list of summary values for CPU statistics for each day of the week. You'll see values for Monday, Tuesday, Wednesday, and so forth. These statistics can be copied and pasted into a spreadsheet and quickly charted, allowing you to visually see how your CPU load correlates with the day of the week. This is a great way to get a visual display of server values over a period of time.

Display Swap Usage in AIX

The *lsps −a* command is used in AIX to display the swap usage for a server. As discussed earlier, an Oracle database server may experience swapping when the SGA is consuming too much of the server's RAM, and the demands of PGA memory cause RAM to be moved onto the swap disk.

In the following example, you would have swapping if any of the paging disks showed write activity in the %Used column:

```
root>lsps -a

Page Space  Phys Vol    Volume  Gr Size...
paging00    hdisk3      maxvg     40MB...
hd6         hdisk0      rootvg  2048MB...

...%Used Active  Auto  Type
...    0     no    no    lv
...    3    yes   yes    lv
```

In this example, the *paging00* disk has a %Used value of zero, which indicates that no paging is taking place.

Display Swap Usage in HP-UX

In HP-UX, the *swapinfo* command is used to display swap usage for a server. In the following example, you can see the swap disk in the row where the type is *dev*: the first line of output represents the swap segment. You can see that one gigabyte of swap space has been allocated to the */dev/gv00/lvol12* logical volume.

```
root>swapinfo -tam

          Mb    Mb   Mb...
TYPE     AVAIL USED FREE...
dev       1024   25  999...
reserve      -  999 -999...
memory    3966 3547  419...
total     4990 4571  419...


... PCT      Mb
... USED RESERVE  PRI  NAME
...   2%       1        /dev/vg00/lvol2
...
...  89%
...  92%       0    -
```

As with AIX, the percent used value for the swap device indicates if swapping is occurring.

Show Server Load Averages

Another way of showing Oracle process usage is to monitor the load average. As mentioned before, the *load average* is an arbitrary number describing the load on the system.

In the following example, the Unix *w* (watch) command is used to generate an abbreviated top sessions output. Most experienced Oracle DBAs use the *w* command to quickly check server load, because *w* is present in almost all dialects of Unix.

```
ROOT>w

10:02AM up 60 days, 18:46, 3 users,
```

```
load average: 0.32, 0.39, 0.43
User      tty      login@  idle   JCPU   PCPU  what
oracle    pts/0    08:17AM    0  80:18  80:16  w
oracle    pts/1    09:15AM    5      2      0  ftp
miltonrv  pts/2    01May00  9days     0      0  -ksh
```

Note that there are three values for the load average (which follows the time and user count). These are the load averages for the past minute (0.32), the past 5 minutes (0.39), and the past 15 minutes (0.43). Whenever the load average value exceeds 1, you have a CPU overload problem.

Use iostat

The *iostat* utility shows elapsed I/O against each of the physical disks. The following example shows *iostat* being used. The command-line parameter 3 represents the time interval in seconds between snapshots. The numbers reported are those accumulated during each three-second interval.

```
ROOT>iostat 3

tty:    tin    tout  %user  %sys  %idle  %iowait
        0.0   306.7   10.3   0.7   81.7      7.3

Disks: tm_act   Kbps  tps  Kb_read  Kb_wrtn
hdisk5    0.0    0.0  0.0        0        0
hdisk6    0.0    0.0  0.0        0        0
hdisk0    4.7   20.0  5.0       60        0
hdisk1    0.0    0.0  0.0        0        0
hdisk2    0.0    0.0  0.0        0        0
hdisk3    0.0    0.0  0.0        0        0
hdisk4    2.7   12.0  3.0       36        0
hdisk7    0.0    0.0  0.0        0        0
```

The important columns in the *iostat* output are:

Kb_read
   The number of kilobytes read during the elapsed interval

Kb_wrtn
   The number of kilobytes written during the elapsed interval

The *iostat* utility is great for finding busy disks. When the wait CPU percentage (the *wa* column) reported by *vmstat* indicates an I/O bottleneck, running the *iostat* utility should be your next step. I/O bottlenecks are identified by wait queues for access to the disk. You can therefore find busy disks by checking *iostat* for high read/write activity. Next, identify the corresponding mount point (get the mapping of disk to mount points from your system administrator). Once you have the mount point, you can run Oracle's *utlbstat-utlestat* scripts to determine the specific Oracle data files that are causing the bottleneck. Once you identify them, you can move them onto a "cooler" disk, or stripe them across several devices.

Automate iostat Collection

Most I/O activity in an Oracle database is very sporadic and transient. To get an accurate picture of I/O activity by disk, you can create a Unix script to capture the output of *iostat* and place it into Oracle tables for later analysis. This section shows you a set of tables and a script that you can use to capture I/O statistics.

cr_iostat_tab.sql

The upcoming script (which you could name *cr_iostat_tab.sql*) creates three tables that I use when collecting *iostat* statistics:

iostat
> Contains the raw statistics as captured from *iostat*

sum_iostat
> Contains statistics that have been summarized by sample date and mount point

vol_grp
> Provides a cross reference between mount points and physical disks

---

The *vol_grp* table is an important cross-reference table that you need to populate manually based on how your disks are partitioned into mount points. The *iostat* utility returns data for physical disks on your system. The *vol_grp* table correlates physical disks to mount points and is used by the query that summarizes the *iostat* data.

```
create table iostat
(
year                number(4),
month               number(2),
day                 number(2),
hour                number(2),
minute              number(2),
hdisk               varchar2(8),
kb_read             number(9,0),
kb_write            number(9,0)
)
tablespace dba_perf
storage (initial 20m next 1m)
;

create table sum_iostat
(
samp_date           date,
mount_point         varchar2(30),
elapsed_seconds     number(4),
kb_read             number(9,0),
kb_write            number(9,0)
)
tablespace dba_perf
storage (initial 10m next 1m )
;

create table vol_grp
(
mount_point         varchar2(30),
vol_grp             varchar2(14),
hdisk               varchar2(8)
)
```

```
tablespace dba_perf
storage (initial 2k next 2k)
;
```

Adjust the tablespace name and storage parameters to suit
your environment.

---

get_iostat.ksh

With the tables created, you can invoke the following script
(which you could name *get_iostat.ksh*) to constantly capture *iostat* information:

```
#!/bin/ksh

SAMPLE_TIME=300
while true
do
    iostat ${SAMPLE_TIME} 2 > /tmp/tmp1
    COUNT=`cat /tmp/tmp1|wc -l `
    COUNT2=`expr $COUNT / 2`

    # This script is intended to run starting
    # at 7:00 AM EST Until midnight EST
    cat /tmp/tmp1|sed 1,${COUNT2}d | awk\
   '{ printf("%s %s %s\n", $1, $5, $6) }'\
  | while read HDISK VMSTAT_IO_R VMSTAT_IO_W
    do
        if (echo $HDISK|grep -cq hdisk );then

        YEAR=`date +"%Y"`
        MONTH=`date +"%m"`
        DAY=`date +"%d"`
        HOUR=`date +"%H"`
        MINUTE=`date +"%M"`

        sqlplus -s / <<EOF
        insert into iostat
         values
```

```
                ( $YEAR,
                  $MONTH,
                  $DAY,
                  $HOUR,
                  $MINUTE,
                  $SAMPLE_TIME,
                  '$HDISK',
                  $VMSTAT_IO_R,
                  $VMSTAT_IO_W);

        delete from iostat
        where kb_read < 10
        and kb_write < 10;
        EXIT
EOF
        fi
    done
    rm /tmp/tmp1

    sqlplus -s / <<EOF

    insert into sum_iostat (
    select
        to_date(to_char(samp_date,
        'YYYY-MM-DD-HH24-MI'),'YYYY-MM-DD-HH24-MI'),
        mount_point,
        $SAMPLE_TIME,
        sum(kb_read),
        sum(kb_write)
    from
        vol_grp a,
        iostat b
    where
        a.hdisk = b.hdisk
    and
    to_char(samp_date,'YYYY-MM-DD-HH24-MI') =
    (select max(to_char(samp_date,
    'YYYY-MM-DD-HH24-MI')) from iostat)
    group by
        to_date(to_char(samp_date,
        'YYYY-MM-DD-HH24-MI'),'YYYY-MM-DD-HH24-MI'),
```

```
      mount_point
   );

   EXIT
EOF
done
```

In this script, you will see a DELETE statement that removes
small-value rows from the statistics. Because of the large
volumes of data collected, it is important to remove data for
files with little or no activity. If you run this script every five
minutes in a database with 100 files, then you will get
28,800 rows per day. You don't want to be deluged with
that much information. That's the reason for removing data
rows for files having only a small amount of activity.

TIP

The *get_iostat.ksh* script uses operating-system authentication to log on to Oracle in order to avoid embedding a username and password in the script.

File Management

Most Oracle DBAs are responsible for the management of
the Oracle data files on their database servers. You must be
able to determine the status of all the Oracle data files, initialization files, trace files, and log files.

List Recently Touched Files

As a DBA, you often need to see the most recently touched
files in a filesystem. An Oracle file is *touched* each time that
the file is read or written. Knowing when a file has been
touched can offer you insight into the behavior of Oracle on
your server. The *ls* command in the following example gen-
erates a sorted list of files, with the most recently accessed
files appearing first. That output is piped through *head* in
order to limit the display to the most recently touched files.

```
>ls -alt|head

-rw-r----- 1 ... 52429312 May 11 07:00 arlog272.arc
-rw-r----- 1 ... 393829   May 10 20:20 arlog21.arc.Z
-rw-r----- 1 ... 19748689 May 10 20:03 arlog27.arc.Z
-rw-r----- 1 ... 16018687 May 10 08:05 arlog26.arc.Z
```

Note that "touched" is different from "changed." A file is touched anytime that the file is read by a process, but a file is only *changed* when it has been written.

TIP

The *−l* option of the *ls* command always causes the modification date to be listed with each file, even when you use the *ls −alt |head* command to see the most recently touched files. The *−t* option causes the output to be sorted by touched date, but the modification date is still the date that is displayed. The *−a* option lists all files in your directory.

List Recently Changed Files

The following example uses a variation of the *ls* command that displays the most recently changed files. The *−c* option causes the list of files to be sorted on the date and time of the most recent change. Note that the *−c* option displays in reverse order, so you must pipe the *ls* output to *tail* in order to see the most recent values.

```
>ls -alc|tail

-rw-r----- 1 ... May 09 05:02 archlog263.arc.Z
-rw-r----- 1 ... May 09 05:03 archlog264.arc.Z
-rw-r----- 1 ... May 10 05:02 archlog265.arc.Z
-rw-r----- 1 ... May 10 05:02 archlog266.arc.Z
-rw-r----- 1 ... May 10 05:02 archlog267.arc.Z
-rw-r----- 1 ... May 10 05:02 archlog268.arc.Z
```

Delete Unchanged Files

The file modification date maintained by Unix can be used as the basis for a command that deletes files that have not been changed during a specified period of time. For example, the following command deletes all archived redo log files that have not been changed during the previous five days:

```
/usr/bin/find $DBA/$ORACLE_SID/arch/arch_prod*.arc
-ctime +5 -exec rm {} \;
```

The key here is the *–ctime +5* parameter to the Unix *find* command. That causes the *find* command to search for files with change dates more than five days in the past.

Display File Sizes in 512-Byte Blocks

Sometimes you need to quickly find large trace or core dump files on your Oracle server. Oracle DBAs need to find dump files, and Oracle developers need to locate the trace files associated with a task abort. To see the size of a data file, use the Unix *du* command. The basic *du* command will display the number of 512-byte chunks within any filesystem. In the following example, you can see the sizes of compressed Oracle archived redo log files:

```
>du -s * |sort -n|tail

31288    archlog269.arc.Z
34000    archlog253.arc.Z
34480    archlog256.arc.Z
35464    archlog252.arc.Z
36696    archlog255.arc.Z
37400    archlog258.arc.Z
37456    archlog263.arc.Z
38576    archlog270.arc.Z
39248    archlog267.arc.Z
102408   archlog272.arc.Z
```

You can also use the *du* command to display the sum of all
files within a directory. The command in the following
example does this, and it also uses the *−k* option to show
the size in kilobytes instead of in 512-byte blocks:

```
root>du -sk /home/oracle

2353     .
```

Locate Files That Contain Certain Strings

You can use a combination of the *find* and *grep* commands to search for a file containing a specific string. For
example, assume that you are trying to locate a script that
queries the *v$session* view. You can issue the command
shown in the following example, and Unix will search your
current directory and all subdirectories, looking in all files
for the text "v$session":

```
>find . -print|xargs grep -i v\$session

./rep/sp2/PAUR.log:select username from v$session
./rep/sp2/PUK.log:select username from v$session
./rep/sp2/res.sql:from v$session
./rep/sp2/res.sql:select username from v$session
...
```

Following is a breakdown of this command that describes how each element contributes to the overall goal:

find .

> Generates a list of all files in the current directory and in all directories underneath the current directory.

–print

> Causes the *find* command to actually display the list of files. This display is piped into *xargs*.

xargs

> Performs the *grep* command for each file displayed by the *find* command.

grep –i v\ $session

> Filters out all lines except those that contain "v$session".

Find Recently Created Files

The *find* command shown in the following example is great for finding files that have been recently added to your server. You can use this command when a filesystem is nearly full, and you need to identify the most recently add-ed files. This example shows files that were created during the past day:

```
root>find . -mtime -1 -print

./afiedt.buf
./dead.letter
./donald1/dtmig
./donald1/dtmig/ins_dss.lst
./donald1/dtmig/nohup.out
./donald1/dtmig/on.lst
./donald1/dtmig/ins_dss.sql
./donald1/dtmig/ins_dss.txt
./repfix/refresh/pcan.lst
```

The details for this command are as follows:

find .

> Finds all files in the current directory and in all directories underneath the current directory

−mtime −1
>   Finds files that are less than one day old

−print
>   Displays the list of files

Find Large Files on a Server

When a Unix filesystem becomes full, you must quickly find all large files on the filesystem. Then you must delete something in order to free up space on the filesystem that is full. Failure to do so can render the Unix operating system unstable and can lead to major server failure.

The following command will cascade through the subdirectories and display all files that are greater than a specified size. In this case, the specified size is 10,000 bytes:

```
>find . -size +10000 -print

./repfix/presmp/stdy_plan_task.dmp
```

With the list of large files in front of you, you may spot one that you can delete in order to free up space. Remember that the *find .* command always begins with your current working directory and works downward. Therefore, choose your working directory appropriately with respect to the filesystem that is full.

Delete Files in Bulk

As a DBA, you sometimes need to remove older files from a filesystem. For example, you may want to remove older archived redo logs from your redo log filesystem in order to free up space for more current logs to be archived. You can do this with the help of the *find* command. The *find* command in the following example will identify all files that are more than seven days old:

```
>find . -mtime +7

./archlog251.arc.Z
./archlog252.arc.Z
```

```
./archlog253.arc.Z
./archlog254.arc.Z
```

Now that you have a list of files, you can use the *find* command's −*exec* argument to execute the *rm* command against each file that is found. For example:

```
find . -mtime +7 -exec rm {} \;
```

You can use this command to automatically remove all files that are more than seven days old. Note that −*exec* functions similarly to the *xargs* command shown earlier in this book.

Delete Old Trace and Audit Files

The following Unix code snippet deletes Oracle trace and audit files that are more than 14 days old. It is especially useful, because it loops through all databases defined in your *oratab* file. For each database listed in *oratab*, this script checks the modification dates of the associated audit and trace files. Those files last modified more than 14 days ago are deleted. By running this script from a *cron* job, you ensure that you never experience a buildup of old files.

TIP

If you are using Solaris, the *oratab* file may be located in */var/opt/oratab*.

```
#!/bin/ksh

for ORACLE_SID in `cat /etc/oratab|\
egrep ':N|:Y'|grep -v \*|cut -f1 -d':'`
do
 ORACLE_HOME=`cat /etc/oratab|\
grep ^$ORACLE_SID:|cut -d":" -f2`
 DBA=`echo $ORACLE_HOME | sed -e\
 's:/product/.*::g'`/admin
 find $DBA/$ORACLE_SID/bdump -name \*.trc \
-mtime +14 -exec rm {} \;
 find $DBA/$ORACLE_SID/udump -name\
```

```
\*.trc -mtime +14 -exec rm {} \;
find $ORACLE_HOME/rdbms/audit -name \*.aud \
-mtime +14 -exec rm {} \;
done
```

Let's examine some of the commands in this script. The first command in the *do* loop retrieves the Oracle home directory for the current Oracle SID:

```
ORACLE_HOME=`cat /etc/oratab|grep ^$ORACLE_SID:|cut -
d':' -f2`
```

The elements of this command are as follows:

cat /etc/oratab
  Lists the contents of the *oratab* file

grep ^ORACLE_SID:
  Finds lines with *ORACLE_SID*, starting at the beginning of the line (^) and ending with a colon (:)

cut −d':'−f2
  Using the colon as a word separator, prints the second value in the line

ORACLE_HOME=
  Assigns the result to the *ORACLE_HOME* variable

The second command in the *do* loop retrieves the Oracle home directory associated with the specified SID:

```
DBA=`echo $ORACLE_HOME | sed -e
's:/product/.*::g'`/admin
```

The elements of this second command are as follows:

echo $ORACLE_HOME
  Displays the value of the *ORACLE_HOME* environment variable

sed −e 's/product/.::g'^admin*
  Runs the string editor to replace the string "product" with "admin"

DBA=
  Assigns the result to the *DBA* variable

The third line in the *do* loop deletes all trace files in the background dump destination directory that are more than 14 days old:

```
find $DBA/$ORACLE_SID/bdump -name \*.trc -mtime +14 -
exec rm {} \;
```

The elements of this command are as follows:

find $DBA/$ORACLE_SID/bdump –name *.trc
> Lists all trace files in the *bdump* directory

–mtime +14
> Restricts the list to files more than 14 days old

–exec rm {} \;
> Pipes these files to the *rm* command

The remaining lines in the *do* loop do the same thing for trace files in the user dump destination and for audit files in the audit directory.

Allocate an Empty File

Use the Unix *touch* command to create an empty file with default ownership and permissions. You would commonly do this to create an empty file to receive output or to pre-set permissions for a file. If you are transitioning into Unix, you might note that the *touch* command is the equivalent of the *IEFBR14* utility on a mainframe. In the following example, *touch* is used to create a new file named *test1.txt*:

```
>touch test1.txt

>ls -al test1*

-rw-r-----   1 oracle   dba          0 Aug 13 09:43
test1.txt
```

Change Default File Permissions

Use the *umask* command to set default file permissions within Unix. The value of *umask* is computed by taking the

---

difference between the server default (usually 777 or 644) and the actual value of *umask* for your Unix user ID. This command allows you to set a default *umask* for the Unix Oracle ID and to control the default permissions for all files created by Oracle.

Understand Unix file permissions

Permissions for Unix files are always recorded in terms of three numeric values. Each of the three values represents permissions granted to a different class of users. The three user classes are:

- The file's owner
- Members of the same Unix group as the file's owner
- All other Unix users

Thus, if a file has a permission value of 751, the 7 applies to the owner, the 5 applies to other Unix users who are members of the owner's group, and the 1 applies to all other users. The obvious question now is, "what do those numbers mean?"

Each digit in a permission value represents the sum of one or more of the values listed in Table 1-3.

Table 1-3. Unix Permission Values

Permission Value	Meaning
4	Read permission
2	Write permission
1	Execute permission

Note that the values shown in Table 1-3 sum to the number 7. Thus, the 7 in 751 grants all privileges to the file's owner. The 5, on the other hand, is the sum of 4 + 1. Therefore, users in the same group as the owner may read and execute the file, but they may not write it. The value 1 indicates that all other users may only execute the file.

You can see the permissions for each file when using the Unix *ls* command. However, the permissions are not shown in their numeric form. For example:

```
root>ls -l test1.tst

-rwxr-x--x    1 oracle    dba           0 Aug 13 09:43
test1.txt
```

The permissions in this example correspond to the value 751, but they are represented by the string *–rwxr-x--x*. You can work from that string to a numeric value as follows:

- Ignore the first dash. It indicates that you are looking at a plain file. A *d* in this location indicates a directory.

rwx

The first group of three characters represents the permissions for the file's owner. The letters *r*, *w*, and *x* correspond to read, write, and execute, respectively. The corresponding numeric values, from Table 1-3, are 4, 2, and 1. Add these values together, and you get 7.

r-x

The second group of three characters represents the permissions for other users in the same group as the owner. In this example, you have only *r* and *x* for read and execute. Take 4, the value for read, and add it to 1, the value for execute, and you have 5.

--x

The third group of three characters represents the permissions for all other Unix users. In this case, only execute access has been granted, and the corresponding numeric value is 1.

Concatenate the three values, and you have 751.

Find the systemwide default file permissions

Here is a quick trick for finding the default system permissions on your database server. Temporarily reset the *umask* to 000, and then create a file using the *touch* command.

The resulting file will inherit the default permissions for your server. For example:

```
root>umask 000
root>touch temp
root>ls -al temp
-rw-r--r--   1 oracle   oinstall        0 Sep 29 19:45
temp
```

If you do the math, you'll see that in this case the default system permissions are represented by the value 644.

Set default permissions for your session

Suppose that on your system, the systemwide default permissions are 777. Suppose also that you don't want your files to be created with those permissions. What do you do? The answer is that you use the *umask* command to specify a value that is used to modify the default permissions when you create a file. The value that you specify with *umask* is essentially subtracted from the systemwide default. Table 1-4 provides a few examples to illustrate this process.

Table 1-4. The Effects of the umask Setting

	Example 1	Example 2	Example 3
Server Default	777	644	777
umask Value	022	022	143
New File Permissions	755	622	637

As Example 1 in Table 1-4 shows, a *umask* setting of 022 removes write permissions for group and other. Files normally created with mode 777 are instead created with mode 755; files created with mode 644 become mode 622.

The following example uses *touch* to create a new file. The default *umask* is 022, which leaves the file with a permission of 755 (owner read/write/execute, all others read-only).

```
>umask 022

>touch test.txt
```

```
>ls -al test.txt

-rw-r-xr-x    1 oracle    dba              0 Aug 13 09:36
test.txt
```

For another example, say you wanted to change the default permissions for all new files created by the Oracle user, such that only the Oracle user could write to them and only members of the DBA group could read them. You would want permissions of 740. To do this, you can reset *umask* to 037:

```
>umask 037

>touch test1.txt

>ls -al test1*

-rw-r-----    1 oracle    dba              0 Aug 13 09:43
test1.txt
```

The *umask* setting affects only new files as they are created. It does not affect permissions on existing files. You also need to execute the *umask* command each time that you log on, so you may want to place it in your *.profile* file.

Change File Ownership

The Unix *chown* (change owner) command can be used to change the current ownership of a file. Sometimes a file is created with the wrong user ID, and you need to change the owner and group attributes.

When you use the *ls –al* command to list the files in a directory, you'll see the owner of those files in the third column of the output. In the fourth column, you'll see the group name. In the following example, you can see *chown* being used to change the ownership of all files from *root:sys* to *oracle:oinstall*:

```
root>ls -al
-rw-------    1 root     sys      ...7:11 .bash_history
drwxr-xr-x   11 root     sys      ...1:49 .dt
-rwxr-xr-x    1 root     sys      ...1:12 .dtprofile
```

```
-rwxr-xr-x    1 root    sys    ...2:00 .dtprofile_orig
-rwxr-xr-x    1 root    sys    ...8:31 .profile
-rwxr-xr-x    1 root    sys    ...3:51 .profile_old
-rw-------    1 root    sys    ...9:50 .sh_history
drwx------    2 root    sys    ...9:02 .solregis
-rw-------    1 root    sys    ...9:26 .TTauthority
-rw-------    1 root    sys    ...1:47 .Xauthority

root>chown oracle:oinstall *

root>ls -al
-rw-------     1 oracle    oinstall ...  .bash_history
drwxr-xr-x   11 oracle    oinstall ...  .dt
-rwxr-xr-x    1 oracle    oinstall ...  .dtprofile
-rwxr-xr-x    1 oracle    oinstall ...  .profile
-rwxr-xr-x    1 oracle    oinstall ...  .profile_old
-rw-------    1 oracle    oinstall ...  .sh_history
drwx------    2 oracle    oinstall ...  .solregis
-rw-------    1 oracle    oinstall ...  .TTauthority
-rw-------    1 oracle    oinstall ...  .Xauthority
```

TIP

Note that you can use the *chown* command with the *−R* option to change file ownership for all files in the directory tree, starting from your current directory.

Change File Permissions

The Unix *chmod* command (pronounced "schmod") is used to change the existing permissions for a file. For example, assume that you want to allow a Unix user in the DBA group to write to your Oracle initialization files. You would start by issuing the *ls −al* command to see the existing permissions on those files:

```
>ls -al

-rw-r--r-- 1 oracle dba  ... configPUM.ora
-rw-r--r-- 1 oracle dba  ... initPUM.ora
```

While you, the owner, have read/write permissions, DBA group members have only read permissions. You need to open up access to the group, and you can do that by changing the permissions to 774. This provides read/write/execute privileges to the owner and group, and read permissions to the rest of the Unix world. Use the *chmod* command as follows to change the permissions of all files in the current directory to 774:

```
>chmod 774 *
```

Now, reissue the *ls –al* command, and you'll see that your file permissions have changed:

```
>ls -al

-rwxrwxr--   1 oracle    dba    ...    configPUM.ora*
-rwxrwxr--   1 oracle    dba    ...    initPUM.ora*
```

The *chmod* command also has a set of plus operators (+) that can be used to add read (+*r*), write (+*w*), or execute (+*x*) permissions to a file. Minus variants (–*r*, –*w*, and –*x*) allow you to remove access. You may find it easier to deal with these operators instead of the raw numbers. The command in the following example revokes execute access to all Korn shell scripts in a directory:

```
>chmod -x *.ksh

>ls -al *.ksh

-rw-r--r--   1 oracle    dba    ...    09:11 a.ksh
-rw-r--r--   1 oracle    dba    ...    09:11 lert.ksh
-rw-r--r--   1 oracle    dba    ...    11:32 back.ksh
-rw-r--r--   1 oracle    dba    ...    09:12 coun.ksh
```

When you want to re-enable your shell scripts, the scripts can be made executable again using the +*x* operator:

```
>chmod +x *.ksh

>ls -al *.ksh

-rwxr-xr-x   1 oracle    dba ...    09:11 a.ksh*
```

```
-rwxr-xr-x   1 oracle   dba ...   09:11 lert.ksh*
-rwxr-xr-x   1 oracle   dba ...   11:32 back.ksh*
-rwxr-xr-x   1 oracle   dba ...   09:12 coun.ksh*
```

Disk Management

Disks exist in Unix as physical volumes and are carved into physical partitions (PPs). These physical partitions are, in turn, assigned to logical volumes. A *logical volume* is a chunk of storage that consists of one or more physical partitions. The logical volumes are then mapped onto Unix mount points. Several logical volumes can be used in a mount point, and a collection of such logical volumes is referred to as a *volume group*. A Unix *mount point* is like a directory name, and is used by you, the Oracle DBA, when allocating Oracle data files.

List Logical Volumes in HP-UX

All logical volumes can be listed in HP-UX using the *df –k* command. The *df –k* command shows each logical volume, and the corresponding mount point. For example:

```
ROOT>df -k

/home(/dev/vg00/lvol5): 20166 total allocated Kb
                         4945 free allocated Kb
                        15221 used allocated Kb
                           75 % allocation used
/opt (/dev/vg00/lvol6):615914 total allocated Kb
                       227403 free allocated Kb
                       388511 used allocated Kb
                           63 % allocation used
/tmp (/dev/vg00/lvol4):64215 total allocated Kb
                        20564 free allocated Kb
                        43651 used allocated Kb
                           67 % allocation used
/u01 (/dev/vg01/u01  ):17580720 total allocated Kb
                       12117048 free allocated Kb
                        5463672 used allocated Kb
                           31 % allocation used
```

The *df −k* command is most often used to see the total space in each mount point and the amount of free space within each mount point. In the previous example, you see that */u01* is defined with a size of 17 gigabytes, and has 12 gigabytes free.

The mount point name is outside the parentheses, while the logical volume name is within the parentheses. To see the logical volumes in a filesystem, you can issue the *lvdisplay* command followed by a logical volume name. For example:

```
ROOT>lvdisplay /dev/vg00/u01

--- Logical volumes ---
LV Name                 /dev/vg00/lvol3
VG Name                 /dev/vg00
LV Permission           read/write
LV Status               available/syncd
Mirror copies           1
Consistency Recovery    MWC
Schedule                parallel
LV Size (Mbytes)        140
Current LE              35
Allocated PE            70
Stripes                 0
Stripe Size (Kbytes)    0
Bad block               off
Allocation              strict/contiguous
IO Timeout (Seconds)    default
```

The following *lsvg −o* command can be used to display a list of volume groups with Unix mount points:

```
>lsvg -o

appvg16
appvg15
appvg11
```

Now that you can see the volume groups, you can drill-in using *lsvg −l* to see details for a specific volume group:

```
>lsvg -l appvg01
```

```
appvg01:
LV NAME    TYPE      LPs   PPs   PVs...
loglv00    jfslog      1     1   1...
lv01       jfs       123   123   1...
lv17       jfs        62    62   1...

...   LV STATE     MOUNT POINT
...   open/syncd   N/A
...   open/syncd   /u01
...   open/syncd   /leg
```

You can even get fancy and use the *xargs* command to display the details for all volume groups in the list. For example:

```
>lsvg -o|xargs lsvg -l

LV NAME    TYPE      LPs   PPs   PVs...
loglv15    jfslog      1     1   1...
lv16       jfs       489   489   1...

...   LV STATE     MOUNT POINT
...   open/syncd   N/A
...   open/syncd   /u16

appvg15:
LV NAME    TYPE      LPs   PPs   PVs...
loglv14    jfslog      1     1   1...
lv15       jfs       489   489   1...

...   LV STATE     MOUNT POINT
...   open/syncd   N/A
...   open/syncd   /u15

appvg14:
...
```

Display Unix Mount Points

A mount point is a Unix location of disk storage. There are two main commands to display logical volumes and mount points: *bdf* and *df*.

Display mount points in HP-UX

The *bdf* command is used in HP-UX to display the logical volumes and mount points for each filesystem. For example:

```
>bdf
```

Filesystem	kbytes	used	avail...
/dev/vg00/lvol3	86016	31833	50828...
/dev/vg00/lvol1	47829	22369	20677...
/dev/vg00/lvol8	716800	41675	282595...
/dev/vg00/lvol7	536576	36918	156950...
/dev/vg02/lvol12	9216000	336	8636853...
/dev/vg02/lvol11	4096000	210	3838035...

	%used	Mounted on
...	39%	/
...	52%	/stand
...	60%	/var
...	70%	/usr
...	0%	/u18
...	0%	/u17

Display mount points in AIX and Solaris

In AIX and Solaris, the *df* command is used to display mount points. For example:

```
>df -k
```

Filesystem	1024-blks	Free	%Used...
/dev/hd4	32768	11636	65%...
/dev/hd2	802816	15920	99%...
/dev/hd9var	49152	28316	43%...
/dev/hd3	32768	14420	56%...
/dev/hd1	131072	20484	85%...
/dev/lv01	2015232	843328	59%...
/dev/lv02	2015232	247172	88%...
/dev/lv03	4521984	944420	80%...
/dev/lv04	4505600	1646880	64%...

	Iu	%Iu	Mounted on
...	2017	13%	/

...	26308	14%	/usr
...	567	5%	/var
...	285	4%	/tmp
...	5611	18%	/home
...	5750	2%	/u01
...	916	1%	/u02
...	199	1%	/u03
...	53	1%	/u04

Manage Dialect Differences for Filesystems

As you can see after reading the preceding sections, it can be quite difficult to remember all of the different commands relating to the display of Unix filesystems under different dialects. You can make your life easier by encapsulating these differences into a script.

The following script will store the command to display mount points in a Unix variable named *$dialect_df*. The precise command that is stored depends upon the dialect of Unix that you are using. This technique is very handy if you want to make generalized Unix scripts that run on different Oracle servers (note that OSF1 is the older name for Tru64 Unix).

```ksh
#!/bin/ksh
#**************************************************
# Set up the dialect changes for
# HP-UX and AIX (df -k) vs (bdf)
#**************************************************
os=`uname -a|awk '{ print $1 }'`
if [ $os = "OSF1" ]
then
    dialect_df="df -k"
fi
if [ $os = "AIX" ]
then
    dialect_df="df -k"
fi
if [ $os = "IRIX64" ]
```

```
then
    dialect_df="df -k"
fi
if [ $os = "HP-UX" ]
then
    dialect_df="bdf"
fi
```

In this example, the *os* variable is set using the *uname* command, and that variable is then referenced to determine the specific Unix operating system variant being used. The proper command for the operating system in question is then placed into the *dialect_df* variable. This script properly handles AIX, IRIX64, HP-UX, and OSF1. You can easily extend it to handle other operating systems.

The specific example illustrated here deals with the commands used to list mount points. However, the same technique can easily be extended to other problem domains.

Show Mount Points for a Physical Disk in AIX

To be effective, you, as the Oracle DBA, should know the mapping between physical disks, logical volumes, and mount points. Without this information, it is very difficult to find an I/O problem. In an earlier section, you saw how to use the *iostat* command to find physical disks that have excessive I/O. To map a physical disk to logical volumes and mount points, you can use the *lspv* command:

```
>lspv -l hdisk7

hdisk7:
LV NAME LPs PPs DISTRIBUTION          MOUNT POINT
loglv05   1   1 00..01..00..00..00    N/A
lv06    275 275 00..107..108..60..00  /u06
```

Here, you can see that the physical disk *hdisk7* is associated with the following logical volumes:

```
loglv05
lv06
```

The first logical volume has no mount point. The second logical volume is associated with the mount point /u06.

Miscellaneous Shell Scripts

The topics in this section deal with miscellaneous Unix commands and scripts that are useful for Oracle DBAs.

Create a Soft Link for a File

It is important to have a single *tnsnames.ora* file on each server. This is because database servers with multiple Oracle homes will have many default locations for the *tnsnames.ora* file. For example, each home will have its own *$ORACLE_HOME/network/admin* directory. The resulting proliferation of files can cause some confusion. The ideal is to create a single *tnsnames.ora* file for the database server with soft links pointing from every *$ORACLE_HOME/network/admin* directory to the single copy.

Oracle uses the following search order for finding the *tnsnames.ora* file:

1. *$TNS_ADMIN*

2. */etc* (or */var/opt/oracle* for Solaris)

3. *$ORACLE_HOME/network/admin*

Most AIX and HP-UX sites keep a single copy of the *tnsnames.ora*, *oratab*, *sqlnet.ora*, and *listener.ora* files in the */etc* directory. Under Solaris, these files are kept in */var/opt/oracle*.

Even though the search path will look in */etc* anyway, it is good practice for you to soft-link all such configuration files to */etc*. This removes the possibility of the wrong file being accessed, and shows that you have made an effort to consolidate the common Oracle files.

The following script will create a soft link to *etc* for every
database on the server:

```
# Loop through each database name
# on the host /etc/oratab.
for db in `cat /etc/oratab|egrep ':N|:Y'|\
grep -v \*|cut -f1 -d':'`
do
  # Get the ORACLE_HOME for each database.
  home=`cat /etc/oratab|egrep ':N|:Y'|\
grep -v \*|grep ${db}|cut -f2 -d':'`
  echo " "
  echo "database is $db"
  cd $home/network/admin
  ln -s /etc/tnsnames.ora\
        $home/network/admin/tnsnames.ora
done
```

TIP

Some sites require the root user to initially create the
tnsnames.ora file and change the permissions to allow the
Oracle Unix user to alter the file. You should have your system administrator do this prior to running this script.

Make a Tape Backup Using tar

Unix has a native utility called *tar* for rapid copying of files
to tape archives. Here is an example showing *tar* being
used to do a simple Oracle backup to tape:

```
#!/bin/ksh

echo Start `date`

#**********************************************
# Mount the tape and rewind
#**********************************************
mt -f /dev/rmt/2m rew

#**********************************************
```

```
# Copy directories onto /dev/rmt/2m
#***********************************************
tar cvf /dev/rmt/2m /u01/oradata/PRODDB\
 /u02/oradata/PRODDB

echo End `date`
```

Note that the *mt* command specifies the *rew* parameter, which means that the tape will be rewound after use.

Copy tnsnames.ora to All Unix Servers

This section shows a very useful Unix code snippet that distributes common files to a list of servers. This script requires that the *.rhosts* file be set up to allow *rcp* (remote copy) and *rsh* (remote shell) commands. It also uses a driving file called *dbnames* that contains hostname/database name pairs.

The script in this example copies your *tnsnames.ora* file to all hosts listed in the *dbnames* file:

```
#!/bin/ksh

echo 'starting distr'

# Note: dbnames file is in the form HOST DATABASE.
for host in `cat dbnames|awk '{ print $1 }'`
do
    db=`cat dbnames|awk '{ print $2 }'`
    echo        starting distr to $host
    rcp -p tnsnames.ora $host:/etc/tnsnames.ora
    rsh $host ls -al /etc/tnsnames.ora
done
```

Test for a Dead Net8 Listener

One problem with early versions of Net8 is that the listener process will sometimes crash, or it will lock up and refuse to accept database connections. In these cases, a Unix

---

script can be created to detect when a listener is refusing connections and then automatically restart the listener:

```ksh
#!/bin/ksh
# See if listener is running.
lsnr_up=`ps -eaf |grep lsnr |grep -v grep |wc -l`

# If not, see if database is running.
if test $lsnr_up -eq 0 then
        pmon_up=`ps -eaf |grep -i pmon |\
grep -v grep |wc -l`
        smon_up=`ps -eaf |grep -i smon |\
grep -v grep |wc -l`
        dbwr_up=`ps -eaf |grep -i ora |grep -i dbw |\
grep -v grep |wc -l`
        lgwr_up=`ps -eaf |grep -i lgwr |\
grep -v grep |wc -l`

        # If database is up, restart listener.
        if test $pmon_up -gt 0 &&
           test $smon_up -gt 0 &&
           test $dbwr_up -gt 0 &&
           test $lgwr_up -gt 0
           then # Oracle is up
           lsnrctl start $1 #  Start tnslsnr
           echo 'Started tnslsnr ' `date`
        fi
fi
```

Exit a Script When the Database Is Not Running

You can use the set of commands shown in this section to make a Unix script terminate if a specified condition is met. In the example that follows, the script exits if the database is not running. The code checks for the existence of the PMON process for the database instance (which should exist if the database is running), and exits if that process is not found.

```
#!/bin/ksh
#********************************************
# Let's exit immediately if the
# database is not running.
#********************************************
check_stat=`ps -ef|grep ${ORACLE_SID}|\
grep pmon|wc -l`;
oracle_num=`expr $check_stat`
if [ $oracle_num -lt 1 ]
 then
 exit 0
fi
```

Detect When Oracle Is Not Accepting Connections

One of the best ways to detect when the Net8 listener is
having problems is to have a Unix script attempt to connect through the listener. The following script does this by
invoking SQL*Plus to execute a simple SQL query:

```
#!/bin/ksh
#**************************************************
# Test to see if Oracle is accepting connections.
#**************************************************
$ORACLE_HOME/bin/sqlplus -s /<<!\
 > /tmp/check_$ORACLE_SID.ora
select * from v\$database;
exit
!

#**************************************************
# If not, exit immediately.
#**************************************************
check_stat=`cat /tmp/check_$ORACLE_SID.ora|\
grep -i error|wc -l`;
oracle_num=`expr $check_stat`
if [ $oracle_num -gt 0 ]
 then
 exit 0
fi
```

```
# Here you place your alert message.
#********************************
# Mail Alert File
#********************************

cat /usr/alert_message_for_DBA.lst|mailx -s\
 "DBA Alert Summary" michael.dunbar@corp.com\
 donald.burleson@corp.com joe.schmoe@corp.com\
 jonathan.gennick@corp.com
```

The *if* statement causes this script to exit with a success status if SQL*Plus was able to connect. Otherwise, control drops through to the bottom of the script where you can place whatever code you need to notify you of the problem.

Mail ORA-600 Errors from the Alert Log to the DBA

The following commands will collect all ORA-600 error messages from the alert log and then mail them to you. This is a very useful script if you want to keep track of unusual messages in the alert log.

```
#***************************************************
# Mail ORA-00600 messages to the DBAs
#***************************************************

dbalist='burleson@frontiernet.net\
 Don@remote-dba.net'

cat alert_$ORACLE_SID.log|grep 0600|mailx -s\
 "$ORACLE_SID alert log message detected" $dbalist
```

Schedule Tasks with cron

One nice utility that is available in most Unix dialects is the *cron* utility. The term *cron* is short for "chronological"—the *cron* utility allows you to create and schedule tasks for execution at specific times.

The *cron* utility uses a special file known as the *crontab* file to keep track of jobs that you schedule. There are two main *cron* commands you'll need to be aware of:

crontab –l

　　Lists the *crontab* file, allowing you to see what jobs you have scheduled

crontab –e

　　Invokes an editor on the *crontab* file, allowing you to make changes

---

TIP

You may need your system administrator to set up permissions allowing the Oracle Unix user to execute *cron*.

View currently scheduled jobs

In the following example, *crontab –l* is used to list the contents of the current *crontab* file for the Oracle Unix user:

```
>crontab -l
#**********************************************
# Daily Cleanup Tasks of old trace,
# audit, and log files
#**********************************************
00 6 * 2 * /usr/local/bin/scripts/cleanup.ksh > /usr/
local/bin/scripts/cleanup.log
#**********************************************
# Shutdown of Oracle APPS
#**********************************************
00 2 * * * /usr/local/bin/scripts/apps_stop.ksh PROD >
/usr/local/bin/scripts/logs/apps_stop_PROD
05 2 * * * /usr/local/bin/scripts/apps_stop.ksh TEST >
/usr/local/bin/scripts/logs/apps_stop_TEST
#**********************************************
# Shutdown of Oracle Databases
#**********************************************
```

```
30 2 * * * /usr/local/bin/scripts/database_stop.ksh
PROD > /usr/local/bin/scripts/logs/database_stop_PROD
40 2 * * * /usr/local/bin/scripts/database_stop.ksh
TEST > /usr/local/bin/scripts/logs/database_stop_TEST
```

TIP

The Unix user named *oracle* owns the *crontab* entries that control scheduled database jobs.

You can see that there's a structure to *crontab* entries. Each entry is one line, and each line begins with five elements separated by spaces. These elements are usually numeric, and they control the execution time of each entry. Immediately following the five time elements, you have the command to be executed. Following the command are any needed parameters. The five execution-time elements are defined, in the order in which they appear, as follows:

minute
  The minute of the hour (0-59)

hour
  The hour of the day (0-23)

monthday
  The day of the month (1-31)

month
  The month of the year (1-12)

weekday
  The day of the week (0=Sunday, 1=Monday, . . . 6=Saturday)

For entries where all values apply, use an asterisk (*) as a wildcard. For example, to schedule a job to run on each day of the week, use * for the weekday value. Let's look at the first two entries in our *crontab* file and examine more closely how all this works. Note that each *crontab* line

---

wraps, so two lines in the book represent one line in the *crontab* file:

```
00 6 * 2 * /usr/local/bin/scripts/cleanup.ksh > /usr/
local/bin/scripts/cleanup.log
...
00 2 * * * /usr/local/bin/scripts/apps_stop.ksh PROD >
/usr/local/bin/scripts/logs/apps_stop_PROD
```

Here you see that *cleanup.ksh* is scheduled for execution on day 2, hour 6, and minute 00. The monthday and month fields are asterisks (*), so they don't matter. Day 2 is Tuesday, so *cleanup.ksh* will run every Tuesday at 6:00 A.M.

The *apps_stop.ksh* script in this example has * for its weekday value, so it will run every day. The hour and minute values are 2 and 00 respectively, so the script will run daily at 2:00 A.M. The *cron* utility always uses a 24-hour clock, with 00 representing midnight.

Schedule a new job

To add a new job to your Oracle schedule, you can use the *crontab −e* (edit) command. The *crontab −e* command extracts the *crontab* file into the *vi* editor, where you can add a new line for a new job. Once saved, this file will then be activated, and your new job will run as scheduled.

Index of Commands

More Titles from O'Reilly

Oracle

Oracle SQL*Plus: The Definitive Guide

By Jonathan Gennick
1st Edition March 1999
526 pages, ISBN 1-56592-578-5

This book is the definitive guide to SQL*Plus, Oracle's interactive query tool. Despite the wide availability and usage of SQL*Plus, few developers and DBAs know how powerful it really is. This book introduces SQL*Plus, provides a syntax quick reference, and describes how to write and execute script files, generate ad hoc reports, extract data from the database, query the data dictionary tables, use the SQL*Plus administrative features (new in Oracle8i), and much more.

Oracle Essentials: Oracle8 & Oracle8i

By Rick Greenwald, Robert Stackowiak & Jonathan Stern
1st Edition October 1999
374 pages, ISBN 1-56592-708-7

This concise guide explains what's important about Oracle8 (the "object-relational database") and Oracle8i (the "Internet database"). It covers overall system products, architecture, and data structures; installation, management, security, networking, backup and recovery, and tuning issues; and specific technologies such as data warehouses, online transaction processing (OLTP), distributed systems, high availability, Oracle8 and Oracle8i extensions, and Oracle's interfaces to the Web.

Oracle SQL*Plus Pocket Reference

By Jonathan Gennick
1st Edition April 2000
94 pages, ISBN 1-56592-941-1

This quick reference is an excellent, portable resource for every Oracle administrator and developer. It summarizes the syntax of SQL*Plus, Oracle's ubiquitous interactive query tool, including new Oracle8i release 8.1.6 features. It also summarizes how to interact with SQL*Plus and presents the basics of selecting data, formatting reports, and tuning SQL.

O'REILLY®

TO ORDER: **800-998-9938** • order@oreilly.com • http://www.oreilly.com/
OUR PRODUCTS ARE AVAILABLE AT A BOOKSTORE OR SOFTWARE STORE NEAR YOU.
FOR INFORMATION: **800-998-9938** • 707-829-0515 • info@oreilly.com

Oracle

Oracle Database Administration: The Essential Reference

By David Kreines & Brian Laskey
1st Edition April 1999
580 pages, ISBN 1-56592-516-5

This book provides a concise reference to the enormous store
of information Oracle8 or Oracle7 DBAs need every day. It covers DBA
tasks (e.g., installation, tuning, backups, networking, auditing, query
optimization) and provides quick references to initialization parameters,
SQL statements, data dictionary tables, system privileges, roles, and syntax
for SQL*Plus, Export, Import, and SQL*Loader.

Oracle8i Internal Services for Waits, Latches, Locks and Memory

By Steve Adams
1st Edition October 1999
132 pages, ISBN 1-56592-598-X

Based on Oracle8i, release 8.1, this concise book contains detailed,
hard-to-find information about Oracle internals (data structures,
algorithms, hidden parameters, and undocumented system statistics).
Main topics include waits, latches, locks (including instance locks used
in parallel server environments), and memory use and management.
Aimed especially at readers doing advanced performance tuning.

Oracle SAP Administration

By Donald K. Burleson
1st Edition November 1999
214 pages, ISBN 1-56592-696-X

This book provides tried-and-true advice for administrators and
developers who use the SAP business system and the Oracle database
system (Oracle8 or Oracle7) in combination. It covers SAP's SAPDBA and
SAPGUI utilities and describes effective data file placement, initialization
parameters, and monitoring techniques, as well as high-performance table
reorganization, backup, recovery, tuning, and parallel processing.